A SHORT HISTORY OF
CANADA

DONALD C. MASTERS

Professor of History
Bishop's University, Lennoxville, Quebec

AN ANVIL ORIGINAL
under the general editorship of
LOUIS L. SNYDER

ROBERT E. KRIEGER PUBLISHING COMPANY
HUNTINGTON, NEW YORK
1980

To My Wife

Original Edition 1958
Reprint Edition 1980

Printed and Published by
ROBERT E. KRIEGER PUBLISHING COMPANY, INC.
645 NEW YORK AVENUE
HUNTINGTON, NEW YORK 11743

Copyright © 1958 by
Donald C. Masters
Reprinted by Arrangement with
D. VAN NOSTRAND COMPANY, INC.

Printed in the United States of America

Library of Congress Cataloging in Publication Data

Masters, Donald Campbell, 1908-
    A short history of Canada.

    Reprint of the edition published by Van Nostrand,
Princeton, N.J., in series: An Anvil original.
    Bibliography: p.
    Includes index.
    1. Canada—History.   I. Title.
[F1026.M43 1980]   971   80-12913
ISBN 0-89874-201-3

PREFACE

This volume traces Canada's story from the beginnings of colonization in the seventeenth century to its emergence as a nation in the twentieth century. The attempt has been made to produce a well-balanced history in which the political, economic, social, religious and cultural aspects of Canadian development each receive an appropriate measure of emphasis. Social life, particularly the springs of action arising out of thought and belief, are sometimes ignored in histories of Canada. These little known phases of Canadian life have been condensed and included, as well as the better known political and economic factors. The volume places Canada in its proper setting in world affairs, indicating the European and North American origins of Canadian civilization and tracing the long story of Canada's relations with Great Britain and with the United States. The readings provide informative and, at times, colorful material to support and illuminate the narrative.

The volume is intended for all those people who desire some knowledge of the historical background, traditions, problems and achievements of the Canadian people. It is hoped that it will be of particular value to certain specific groups. Among these are (1) university students taking courses in history and in other subjects in which a knowledge of Canada's history is an important cognate feature; (2) students who are not specializing in history or in other social sciences but who desire a brief factual and interpretative account of the Canadian story; (3) high school teachers in history and the social sciences; (4) recent or prospective immigrants to Canada; (5) business men in the United States and elsewhere, who are interested in the Canadian market and investment field and who therefore desire an awareness of the Canadian background; (6) students in business schools; (7) American military personnel.

I wish to acknowledge my debt of gratitude to Dr. Louis L. Snyder, the general editor of the Anvil Books, for his kind encouragement and constructive criticism.

Bishop's University,   D. C. MASTERS
Lennoxville, P. Q.

TABLE OF CONTENTS

Part 1

A SHORT HISTORY OF CANADA

— 1 —

INTRODUCTION

Canada's European Background. For the purposes of this volume Canadian history may be regarded as commencing with the arrival of European explorers and settlers in North America in the sixteenth and seventeenth centuries. The beginnings of white settlement in North America were part of a tremendous process of transition which marked the change in Europe from the mediaeval to the early stages of the modern world. Its economic aspect, which has been called the Commercial Revolution, was marked by a vast extension and reorganization of the European economy. Trade and commerce, industry, agriculture, and other elements of the European economy were expanded and came largely under the control of individual entrepreneurs, the new middle class. Increases in production, in such industries as that of wool, created surpluses for export and a desire for foreign markets. There was an increased desire to secure more cheaply the luxury goods of the East such as spices, drugs, dyestuffs, and silks. The capitalist revolution provided powerful incentives to voyages of exploration to North America and was in turn stimulated by the results which the voyages produced.

The transition period consisted not only of material changes but also involved important developments in thought. The efflorescence of learning and the arts which we call the Renaissance had far-reaching effects in Europe and in America: it provided the explorers with essential knowledge and helped to stimulate their desire to open up hitherto uncharted areas of the earth. The Protestant

Reformation which divided Europe into warring camps provided the incentive which induced thousands of settlers to cross the ocean and to seek a home which would be free from religious persecution. Accompanying these developments went the rise of the so-called nation states, reasonably compact centralized countries, like England, France, and Spain which gradually displaced the older political system based upon the primacy of the Pope and the Holy Roman Emperor. It was chiefly these three nations which supported the early explorers and which utilized their discoveries in order to establish colonies.

The Canadian Scene. Canadian history, like that of the Americas in general, has been largely the story of the interaction between European culture and the North American environment. The early Canadian explorers encountered a country which consisted of three great mountainous formations: the Appalachians, the Laurentian Shield, and the Cordillera or Rockies; and two plains: the St. Lawrence Valley and the great central plain. There were two great indentations, the St. Lawrence-Great Lakes system and the Hudson and James Bay. As Europeans approached the country from the east, they found that it was suited by soil and climate for European settlement. It was capable of rapid penetration by way of the St. Lawrence and by Hudson Bay. It produced staples: fish, furs, timber, and agricultural produce, capable of supporting settlement. The Laurentian region, while unsuited for agriculture, could be used for transportation, which became an increasingly important factor in the fur trade.

Beginnings of Exploration. During the sixteenth and seventeenth centuries much of eastern Canada was explored and some of it settled. As early as the tenth and eleventh centuries, the Norsemen, notably Leif Ericson, had ranged along the eastern coasts of North America, but they had established no permanent settlements. Nor did the European fishermen, who probably operated on the Grand Banks in the fourteenth and fifteenth centuries. Exploration of the Canadian mainland followed the "discovery" of North America by Columbus in 1492. The early explorers of Canada were French and English. Principal among them were John Cabot, who discovered

Newfoundland and the adjacent fishing areas in 1497; Jacques Cartier (1491-1557), who explored the Gulf of St. Lawrence and the river up to the site of Montreal in three voyages (1534, 1535, 1541); Henry Hudson who entered Hudson and James Bay in 1610; and Samuel de Champlain (1567?-1635), who penetrated the region, now eastern Ontario, bounded by the Ottawa River, Lake Nipissing, Georgian Bay, Lake Ontario, the St. Lawrence River, and the Iroquois country south of Montreal and east of Lake Ontario in the years 1609-1615. (*See Reading No. 1.*)

Subsequent exploration of the interior of the continent was achieved by Pierre Esprit Radisson (1636?-1710?) and his brother-in-law, Chouart Des Groseillers (1625-1685), who explored territory west of the Great Lakes probably in the years between 1654 and 1660; Louis Jolliet (1645-1700) and Fr. Jacques Marquette (1637-1675), who set out from Green Bay on Lake Michigan and travelled down the Mississippi to its junction with the Arkansas in 1673; and Sieur de La Salle (1643-1687), who descended the Mississippi from its junction with the Illinois and reached its mouth in 1682. Pierre de la Vérendrye (1685-1749), the great explorer of the western Canadian prairies, set out from Montreal in 1731 and in the next ten years built a chain of fur-trading posts at Rainy Lake, the Lake of the Woods, Lake Winnipeg, the Red River, and on the Assiniboine River. In 1738 he visited the Mandan villages on the Missouri. In 1742 two of his sons penetrated far to the southwest, and possibly reached the foothills of the Rocky Mountains.

The motives which impelled the explorers to undertake these dangerous voyages into the unknown may be suggested: sheer curiosity combined with the desire for personal honour and economic gain. The latter was expected to follow the discovery of direct communications with the Far East or of richer fur-trading areas. The Jesuits who helped to open up southern Ontario after Champlain's explorations were primarily motivated by the desire to convert the Indians. While the French were exploring the continent, they were establishing for themselves a great North American empire, destined to last until the British conquest in 1759-1760. The English, too, established a foothold in what is now Canada with the commencement of trading activities by the Hudson's Bay Company, which was chartered in 1670.

— 2 —

FRENCH RULE, 1604-1760

Settlement. French colonization in Canada was a by-product of the fishing and fur industries. It began with the establishment of short-lived settlements on the Island of St. Croix in 1604 and in 1605 at Port Royal, in what is now the Annapolis Basin in Nova Scotia. Quebec was founded by Champlain in 1608. Gradually, settlement lengthened out along the shores of the St. Lawrence and the Richelieu. The only period of vigorous state assistance to immigration occurred under the great intendant, Jean Talon (1625?-1694). As a result of his energetic policy, the settled population of the colony increased from 3,215 in 1666 to 6,705 in 1673. By the end of the period of French control, New France had a population of between 60,000 and 70,000.

Economic Development. The French were originally attracted to Newfoundland and the region of the St. Lawrence by the fisheries. They developed a prosperous fishing industry based on the south shore of Newfoundland but carried on chiefly in ships from the mother country. They continued this practice to the eighteenth century. The principal competitors of the French were English fishermen, particularly those from the west country ports, and New Englanders, especially after 1650. The fisheries were a source of conflict between France and Great Britain for imperial supremacy in the North Atlantic area.

The principal supporting base of New France was the fur trade. Profits from furs financed government, the church, and, indeed, life itself in the colony. French fishermen began to secure furs from the Indians at Tadoussac in the sixteenth century, and the fur trade gradually became a more important enterprise for the French than the fisheries. In the seventeenth century the French developed an organization in which the marketing of furs was carried on by chartered companies, particularly the Company of New France (1627-1663), but the actual purchase of furs from the Indians was effected by individual traders, the famous *coureurs de bois*. Competition from the English, operating from Albany to the South and from Hudson Bay in the north, drove the French fur traders into the interior of the continent in the search for unmolested fur areas. It also necessitated the construction of forts to defend the lines of communication. By the end of the period, the French were operating in the valley of the Saskatchewan, as well as the Great Lakes area and in the valley of the Mississippi and its tributaries. They had developed a whole network of forts designed to prevent English expansion by shutting in the English along the Atlantic seaboard and on Hudson Bay.

The fur trade that provided the driving force behind French exploration of the continent also confronted the colony with grave problems. The industry was embarrassed by increasing costs, which were partly a result of English competition. The English menace raised the overhead by necessitating heavy commitments in soldiers and forts. The expenses of transportation rose as the trade was driven into the interior. The concentration upon furs prevented any extensive diversification of the economy by diverting men and capital from agriculture and industry.

Despite the retarding effects of the fur trade, the French managed to develop the peasant economy of the *seigneuries,* or French feudal estates. They produced such crops previously known in France as wheat, oats, corn, barley, hemp, and flax; and Indian crops like tobacco, corn, and squash. The colony developed some industry including sawmills, shipyards, and an ironworks at Three Rivers. All these aspects of the economy suffered from the exhausting effects of the fur trade. Yet, it was this settled part of the economy which was destined to last and give to the French way of life in New France its characteristic features: feudalism and a settled ecclesiastical organization.

The Seigneurial System.   French feudalism assumed

a modified form as the seigneurial system in the rural districts of New France. Presiding over the estate or seigneury was the seigneur. The peasants or habitants rendered the customary feudal services: the *cens et rentes, banalités,* and *corvée,* and paid tithes to the church. The possibility of taking to the woods and entering the fur trade placed the habitant in a stronger position than his opposite number in France, and the government often supported the habitants in disputes about their obligations to the seigneurs. The seigneur was a much more middle-class type than the feudal noble in France. His traditional feudal political obligations largely fell into disuse. The military service in the community was organized by the captain of militia, an able peasant, not by the seigneur. In many cases the seigneurial court did not function. The intendant at Quebec exercised close supervision over the seigneurs. Despite, or perhaps on account of, these modifications of feudalism, the seigneurial system represented a stabilizing influence in the French-Canadian community. (*See Reading No. 2.*)

The Church in New France. The Roman Catholic Church early assumed an integral and powerful position in the colony. It was associated with the expansionist activities of the French in the interior parts of the continent, where the Jesuits carried on their devoted missionary activities among the Indians, particularly the Hurons in the area south of Georgian Bay. The Georgian Bay mission came to a tragic end when the Hurons were virtually wiped out by the Iroquois in 1648 and 1649; but the mission activities continued. At the same time, parishes were organized in the settled communities; there were thirty-six parishes in New France in 1685 and eighty-two in 1721. The two personalities of importance in the French community were the seigneur and the curé. The church soon established control over education in the colony. In this work the Seminary of St. Sulpice, established in Montreal in 1657, and convent schools, such as that of the Ursulines at Quebec, were of prime importance.

The church was under the centralized control of the bishop at Quebec. This was largely a result of the personality and career of the first bishop, Laval (1623-1708), an aristocratic, imperious but devoted man who arrived in the colony as Bishop of Patraea in 1659 and who was made Bishop of Quebec in 1674. Laval not only occupied a position of dominance in organizing the church in Quebec, but also played a powerful role in government. As a member of the council (see below), he constantly championed the position and ideas of the church in opposition to the governor and the intendant. Laval's career as bishop (1659-1688) marked the beginnings of the close association between church and state which has always been a characteristic feature of life in Quebec.

The church in the colony was inspired by the ideas of the Counter-Reformation; it was Puritan in morality and its zeal to proselytize. The church represented a conservative and moral force in New France, as was exemplified by Laval's vigorous efforts to prevent the sale of liquor to the Indians. The exclusion of the Huguenots from the colony was decided upon by the French government in 1627, partly as a result of Jesuit influence. This made the society of New France homogeneous, although it kept out an industrious people who might have strengthened the colonial economy.

Government and Law. Like the fur trade, the church, and the seigneurial system, government in New France was characterized by centralized control. During the early period, it was in the hands of chartered companies, especially the Company of New France (1627-1663). The Company, in exchange for a monopoly of trade and control of the land, undertook to supply services of government, in addition to bringing out from two hundred to three hundred immigrants each year and supplying priests in each settlement. After several modifications in the forties and fifties, company rule was abolished in 1663 and replaced by royal government. The titular head of the government was the governor, usually a military man, one of whose principal functions was to organize defence and relations with the Indians. The intendant, usually a lawyer, had wide administrative, legislative, and legal power. He acted as a check on the power of the governor. The supreme council consisted at first of the governor, the bishop, the intendant, and five appointed councillors; later it included the same triumvirate and also the attorney-general, the registrar, and twelve appointed councillors. The council had administrative duties such as the fixing of prices and the regulation of trade and could act as a court of appeal for all pleas, both civil and criminal. Yet the council was a distinctly subordinate body which lost power to the governor and the intendant in the period between 1663 and 1759. After 1663 the fur trade was controlled by a succession of chartered companies including the West India Company (1664-1674) and the Company of the Indies.

The legal machinery consisted of seigneurial courts, courts at Quebec, Montreal, and Three Rivers, the council and the intendant's court. The law of New France was based upon the Customs of Paris, royal edicts, decrees of the council, and ordinances issued by the intendant. It was more codified than English common law and in that way preferable. French criminal law was no more severe than English criminal law but lacked such safeguards as trial by jury and habeas corpus. The Customs of Paris made little provision for defence of the individual's rights against the state. The French system permitted such practices as arbitrary arrest, secret examination by the crown prosecutor, and the use of torture to stimulate a sluggish memory.

Government in New France was calculated to function in accordance with the ideas of French mercantilism, which insisted that colonies were not ends in themselves but that they existed solely in the interests of the mother country. Despite its subordination to French imperial interests, the governmental system in Canada produced men trained in public speaking and with a knowledge of legal procedure. They adapted themselves readily to British parliamentary methods after the conquest.

The Duel with Great Britain. Throughout its history, New France was a factor in the struggle for power between the French and the English in North America. The conflict in North America was part of the long struggle for world dominance between France and Great Britain, which began towards the end of the seventeenth century and did not end until Waterloo in 1815; but there were local causes of the North American conflict as well. French and English competed for control of the fur trade.

The French fur trade was an obstacle to the westward expansion of English settlement moving out from the Atlantic seaboard. It was this clash of interests which gave to the struggle for the Ohio valley its vital significance. The Roman Catholicism of the French and the Protestantism of the English, especially the New England Puritans, vastly increased the suspicion between the two peoples.

The European wars between French and English, such as King William's War (1688-1697) and the War of the Spanish Succession (1702-1713), had their counterparts in North America. By the Treaty of Utrecht in 1713, the British were given Nova Scotia and had their occupancy of the south shore of Newfoundland and the forts on Hudson Bay confirmed. Having lost Nova Scotia, the French attempted to maintain control of the Gulf of St. Lawrence by the establishment of the fortress of Louisbourg on Cape Breton Island. By a great arc of forts anchored at Quebec and extending through the Great Lakes region and the Mississippi Valley to Louisiana, they also sought to confine the English to the eastern part of the continent. In the middle part of the century the French devoted great attention to the territory around the lower Lakes and particularly the canoe routes connecting Lakes Ontario and Erie with the Ohio and Mississippi regions. This grand strategy soon met opposition. During the War of the Austrian Succession (1740-1748), the New England colonists captured Louisbourg only to have it returned to France in exchange for Madras in 1748. In the Ohio region the French encountered English traders and also land speculators. Organization of the Ohio Land Company by the English in 1749 helped to precipitate hostilities in the next decade. The Seven Years' War (1756-1763) witnessed the final triumph of Great Britain over France in North America. In its early stages, bungling British generalship and the brilliant leadership of the French general, Montcalm (1712-1759), staved off the British offensive against New France. In 1758 the fortunes of war changed with the capture by the British of Forts Frontenac, Duquesne, and Louisbourg. Fort Niagara fell in 1759. In the same year, the army led by James Wolfe (1727-1759), supported by the fleet of Admiral Saunders

(1713?-1775), took Quebec. The surrender of Montreal in 1760 completed the French capitulation.

Many reasons can be suggested for the British victory in North America. During the Seven Years' War the French were weakened by the struggle in Europe, particularly the campaigns against Frederick the Great. In North America, having been drawn into the interior, they were trying to maintain a military establishment which was beyond their power to support. They were confronted with superior British sea power and with the greater economic resources of the British American colonies. The latter had a population of 3,000,000 compared with 65,000 French Canadians. The greater dependence of New France upon its mother country rendered British sea power particularly disastrous to the French. The able Montcalm was hampered and frustrated by the lack of co-operation on the part of the governor, Vaudreuil (1698-1778), and of the intendant, Bigot (b. 1703), a notoriously corrupt official. At this unfortunate juncture in the defense of New France, British military leadership, while scarcely brilliant, was sufficiently effective to bring the war to a triumphant conclusion.

— 3 —

BRITISH NORTH AMERICA, 1760-1867

The Problem of Government 1760-1774. The conquest of Canada confronted the British Government with a problem which the British had not hitherto experienced —how to deal with a people of European extraction who possessed a culture just as old and mature as their own. The *Quebecois* were a people tenacious of their culture, which was essentially French, Catholic, identified with the Quebec of the rural areas, and rooted in the North American environment. The British must work out a scheme of government for this French Catholic people with their authoritarian tradition, which must now be adjusted to the Anglo-Saxon imperial system. The problem was complicated by the fact that the conquest brought to Canada Anglo-Saxons, men who inherited the British tradition of representative self-government, of English common law and of respect for civil liberties. They possessed the restless, dynamic energy of Protestantism.

Early British policy was based on the idea of Anglicizing the French. This was indicated in the Royal Proclamation of October 7, 1763, in the commission appointing James Murray (1721-1794) governor, on November 21, 1763, and in his instructions of December 7, 1763. The policy of Anglicization failed because the governors, Murray and his successor, Guy Carleton (1724-1808), did not apply it. The policy had really been abandoned during the period of military rule (1760-1764). Murray, who got on well with the French, worked with the curés and captains of militia and made efforts, as far as possible to retain French law. Murray continued the same policy of appeasement after the establishment of civil government in 1764. He refused to convene an assembly, which would have been exclusively composed of Protestants, and governed through a council composed of appointees friendly to the French. In 1766 he permitted the appointment of Jean Olivier Briand (1715-1794) as virtual bishop of Quebec with the title of Superintendent of the Roman Catholic Church in Canada. Opposition from the Anglo-Saxon merchants precipitated Murray's resignation in 1766; but his successor, Carleton, carried on the same Francophile policy.

Carleton was anxious to remove the disparity between the policy of the British government and that of the administrators on the spot. He returned to England and secured the passage of the Quebec Act of 1774, which has been hailed as the great charter French-Canadian liberties. (*See Reading No. 3.*) The act designed new oaths to admit Roman Catholics to office; officially recognized the tithe which Roman Catholics were to pay to their own church; provided for government by the governor and council but made no provision for an assembly. The act prescribed that French civil law and English criminal law were to hold the field, side by side. The act was more pleasing to the clergy and the seigneurs than to the habitant; in thus securing the loyalty of the leaders among the French, it stabilized the position of English rule in the colony.

The Empire of the St. Lawrence. While the British authorities were working out a *modus vivendi* with the French Canadians, English-speaking merchants were establishing effective control of the trading empire of the St. Lawrence. The merchants settled in Montreal and were at first small in numbers, about fifty in 1765. They were English, Irish, Scottish, some German, and some American. Mainly they were Protestants. Among their number were James McGill (1744-1813), Alexander Henry (1739-1824), Adam Limburner, and the Frobishers, Benjamin (d. 1787) and Joseph (d. 1810). Some of the group began by selling goods to the army; but the fur trade was the great feature of their commercial empire. They assumed direction of the trade which the French had developed and were soon competing with the Hudson Bay Company and with the merchants who operated from the Atlantic seaboard. The fur trade brought French and

English together in Canada in a great co-operative enterprise.

The merchants engaged in a long, bitter struggle with
the British governors, Murray, Carleton, and Sir Frederick Haldimand (1718-1791), whom they regarded as
pro-French and anti-commercial. Despite quarrels with
officialdom, the merchants prospered. After 1768 when
the home government decided to hand over the fur trade
to the colonies most concerned in it, Montreal extended
its trade at the expense of the Americans, and many
merchants, including Simon McTavish (1750-1804) moved
to Canada. During the years preceding the American War
of Independence, the Canadians pushed into the northwest, where they were displacing the Hudson's Bay Company. The Canadian fur traders moved toward amalgamation in the seventies, and the result was the emergence
of the North West Company in 1783. Montreal suffered
a great blow in the Treaty of Versailles of 1783, which
gave the Americans the Ohio, Mississippi, and much of
the Great Lakes regions. Yet, the North West Company
developed a superb *esprit de corps* and pushed the struggle against the Hudson's Bay Company and the Americans.

The Loyalists.   The nature of the Canadian political
problem was decisively altered by the American War of
Independence, which resulted in the arrival in the British
American colonies of thousands of Loyalists, for the most
part English-speaking and Protestant. The Loyalists came
from every walk of life and from many regions, including
Massachusetts, New York, Virginia, Pennsylvania, and
the Carolinas. They left the United States for a variety
of reasons: persecution, confiscation of land, imprisonment, and also the attractions of good, cheap land in
Canada. The final destinations of the Loyalists were
widely scattered. Many went to Great Britain and the
West Indies. About forty thousand came to British North
America. They were settled in what soon became New
Brunswick, in the Loyalist counties on the north shore
of the St. Lawrence, along the north shore of Lake Ontario west of Kingston, in the Niagara Peninsula, and in
the Amherstburg region. A few remained in the eastern
townships of Quebec. They varied considerably in social
class. The New Brunswick group, which was much the

largest, included many aristocrats such as Duncan Ludlow
(1734?-1808), a former judge of the Supreme Court of
New York, and Ward Chipman, a Harvard graduate who
became solicitor-general of New Brunswick. The emi-
grants to Canada were for the most part humbler types,
artisans and farmers, including the German Palatines and
the Glengarry Highlanders, who were settled north of the
St. Lawrence.

The influence of the Loyalists had a profound effect on
Canadian development. They founded the colony of New
Brunswick, began the opening up of Upper Canada, and
were an important factor in necessitating a reconsidera-
tion of British policy in regard to the Quebec Act. More
significant in the long run were the attitudes which the
Loyalists helped to ingrain in Canadian thinking: an
abiding hatred of Americans and the United States (*see
Reading No. 4*), a fervent affection for Great Britain and
British institutions, and a liking for an aristocratic society
of privilege with themselves as the privileged group.

An Experiment in Separation. The British government attempted to deal with the Loyalist problem by
dividing Quebec. The dominantly Anglo-Saxon section
was organized as Upper Canada and the French part as
Lower Canada. This policy was implemented by the Constitutional Act of 1791 and by an Order in Council of
August 25, 1791. Each colony was given an elective
legislative assembly and an appointive legislative council
and an executive council. Land grants were to be in freehold tenure in Upper Canada and by seigneurial tenure
in Lower Canada, although new grants could be made in
freehold tenure if the occupant desired it. The Act set
aside land equal to one-seventh of future land grants in
the two colonies for the support of "a Protestant clergy."
This was the beginning of the Clergy Reserve question
which produced bitter controversy for the next sixty years.

After 1783 immigration continued to flow into Canada
from the United States. The migration of Loyalists, according to Hansen and Brebner (*The Mingling of the
Canadian and the American Peoples,* New Haven, 1940,
p. 66) "gradually shaded off into a migration of pioneer
farmers whose only motive was the traditional American
search for better lands and a perfect home." According to

a contemporary gazetteer, 80 per cent of the population of Upper Canada in 1812 was of American birth or descent, only a quarter of it Loyalist. After 1815, immigration into the Canadas became dominantly British. Despite the American origins of so many of the settlers in Upper Canada, the War of 1812-1814 temporarily united nearly all sections in both provinces against the United States. Canadian and British successes at Detroit, Queenston Heights, Beaver Dams, Stony Creek, Chrystler's Farm, and Chateauguay provided the basis for a tradition of military achievement in which French and English could take pride. Defeats at Moraviantown, Put-in-Bay, and Plattsburg were soon forgotten. The war did much to foster Canadian nationalism and hostility towards the United States.

Causes of the Rebellions of 1837.   It had been hoped that the Constitutional Act would produce smooth government in the colonies, but shortly after 1800 acrimonious controversies developed in both Upper and Lower Canada. In Lower Canada a combination of racial, economic, and political factors aligned the French, with a few Anglo-Saxon allies, against the English. The French were intent on preserving their culture. Because they were largely excluded from the direction of the staple trades, they were opposed to developmental projects likely to involve increased taxation. Consequently, they were determined to secure control of the provincial finances by their dominance of the Assembly. As the majority group in the Assembly, they were able to pose as democratic and liberal while advocating a policy of economic conservatism. They were opposed by Anglo-Saxon merchants and their friends in the councils. The Anglo-Saxons appeared reactionary because they represented control of government by the minority, although in an economic sense they were progressive. They favoured building projects, especially the construction of canals along the St. Lawrence. For this reason they were determined that control of finances should be maintained by the governor and the councils, both of which they dominated. The struggle assumed the character of a quarrel over finance and was aggravated by the fact that the French Assembly always confronted English councils supported by the governor. The French were led in the Assembly by Louis-Joseph Papineau (1786-1871), an eloquent but fiery and rash personality who became Speaker in 1815.

The element of race was not important in the struggle which developed in Upper Canada; but as in the Lower Province, an urban, merchant, and official class, the so-called Family Compact, was aligned against a rural, backwoods, farming element. The struggle was complicated and embittered by the conflict between religious denominations; the Church of England and the Presbyterians opposed the claims of the Methodists to a share in the Clergy Reserves. As in Lower Canada, the merchant-official class controlled the Executive and Legislative Councils; but the two elements were more evenly balanced in the Assembly than was the case in Lower Canada.

The Family Compact, which included the Allans, the Boultons, the Rideouts, the Chewetts, the Denisons, and the Robinsons, was mainly concentrated in Toronto; but the group had supporters all over the province. Among them particularly were the Anglican clergy, the Orangemen, and many of the more prosperous people such as Colonel Thomas Talbot (1771-1853) and Colonel John Prince (1796-1870). The Family Compact favoured policies of economic expansion: the establishment of banks, canals, and land companies. They espoused the traditional Tory principles of love for the Empire and hatred of French Canadians, Roman Catholics, Americans, and local reformers.

The reformers included at least three distinct groups: moderate reformers like Robert Baldwin (1804-1858); more extreme radicals led by William Lyon Mackenzie (1795-1861), a testy Scot with a tremendous sense of the rights of the common man (*see Reading No. 5*), and the Methodists led by Egerton Ryerson (1803-1882). The reformers were suspicious of the merchants, whose policies, they feared, would involve increases in taxation. They opposed the Family Compact over public improvements, including the Welland Canal. They were hostile to the Bank of Upper Canada and attacked the land monopoly of the Canada Company and Colonel Talbot. Demands for a fairer distribution of the Clergy Reserves

was mainly responsible for the presence of the Methodists
in the reform group. Like their Lower Canadian counterparts, the reformers were influenced by Jacksonian democracy and by English radicalism.

Course of the Rebellions.　Largely as a result of the
factors mentioned above, armed rebellion broke out in
Lower Canada in November, and in Upper Canada in
December, 1837. In Lower Canada, Sir John Colborne's
veterans crushed the French at St. Charles on the Richelieu and at St. Eustache, north of Montreal. In Upper
Canada, Mackenzie's attempt to capture Toronto failed
as a result of bungling by the insurrectionists, the coolness of many of the Methodists, and the rallying of forces
by the Family Compact. There was sporadic rebel activity
in the southwestern part of the province, and raids by the
rebels and their American friends continued into 1838,
but the back of the rebellion had been broken in December of 1837.

The rebellions precipitated important developments in
Canadian history; they set going the train of events which
culminated in the achievement of responsible government
and eventually in confederation. In Lower Canada the
rebellion came to occupy an important place in the French
tradition of mistreatment suffered at the hands of the
Anglo-Saxons.

Durham's Report.　Lord Durham (1792-1840) was
despatched to Canada as governor in 1838 to investigate
conditions which had given rise to the rebellions and to
make recommendations for reform. He was one of a
small British group of colonial reformers who were noted
for their optimism in regard to the future of the Empire.
Durham was an idealist, generous, impatient of obstacles,
but dogged by ill health for a great part of his career.
His sojourn in Canada lasted only from May 29 to November 1, 1838. From the beginning there was friction
between him and the British Government, and he finally
resigned in protest against their failure to defend him in
Parliament. He is famous chiefly for his report on Canada,
which he submitted to the Colonial Office on February 4,
1839. The greater part of the report (*see Reading No. 6*)
was concerned with Lower Canada, where Durham was

horrified by the racial animosity.[1] He maintained that practically all the problems in the colony stemmed from the division between French and English. He believed the division to be aggravated by the constitution, which enabled the English to dominate the Councils and the French, the Assembly. He believed that in Upper Canada the quarrel between the reformers and the Family Compact was similarly aggravated by the constitution. Durham proposed to remedy the situation by uniting Upper and Lower Canada in a single legislative union in which responsible self-government was to be conceded. He believed that union of Upper and Lower Canada would accomplish an objective which he regarded as of central importance, the assimilation of the French Canadian by the Anglo-Saxon group. Durham's report was directly effective in leading to the Act of Union of 1840, which joined Upper and Lower Canada in the Province of Canada. The fact that Durham with his immense prestige advocated responsible government, gave impetus to the movement in Great Britain and Canada. His proposal to assimilate the French, which has always made him a *bête noir* in Quebec, was never seriously attempted.

Responsible Government. The principal achievement in Canada during the first decade of union was the working out of the principle of responsible government. This was a unique Canadian contribution to the development of the modern British Empire since it represented the method by which increasing self-government in the colonies could be achieved without bringing about separation from the Empire. Responsible government may be defined as a system of government in which the executive is responsible to the elected representatives of the people. Its corollary in the British and Canadian systems is that the executive, or cabinet, is a homogeneous

---

[1] The author does not wish to take up any particular position in regard to what is or is not a "race." The term "race" is in common usage in Canada in reference to the French-speaking and English-speaking groups. It is used in this volume in accordance with this common and traditional Canadian usage.

group which acts in a body and resigns when it loses the confidence of the legislature.

The concession of responsible government in Canada was the result of a process in which forces and personalities on both sides of the Atlantic worked together. Its principal advocates in Great Britain were the colonial reformers. It was regarded by the Colonial Office as a matter of simple justice to the colonists after they had been exposed to world competition by the Repeal of the Corn Laws in 1846 and the Navigation Laws in 1849. It was desired in Canada by a combination of groups. They included French *bleus* and *rouges,* Upper Canadian agriculturists in the Mackenzie tradition, and moderate reformers reflecting the ideas of Robert Baldwin and Francis Hincks (1807-1885). These groups combined in the Reform Party, led by Baldwin and Louis Lafontaine (1807-1864), and pressed steadily during the 1840's for the concession of responsible government. The campaign proceeded during the governorships of Lord Sydenham (1799-1841), Sir Charles Bagot (1781-1843), and Sir Charles Metcalfe (1785-1846). In Nova Scotia, Joseph Howe (1804-1873), the great Maritime reformer, began the struggle for responsible government and carried it on against Lieutenant-Governors Sir Colin Campbell (1776-1847) and Lord Falkland (1803-1884). The principle was finally conceded by the British government in 1846 when Sir John Harvey (1778-1852) was lieutenant-governor of Nova Scotia and Lord Elgin (1811-1863) governor-general of British North America. In an epochal despatch of November 3, 1846, Earl Grey (1802-1894), the Colonial Secretary, informed Harvey that he must abide by the advice of his constitutional advisers "since it cannot be too distinctly acknowledged that it is neither possible nor desirable to carry on the government of any of the British provinces in North America in opposition to the opinion of the inhabitants." It remained for this principle to be worked out in practice in Canada in a time of crisis in 1849.

The Elgin Administration. The period of Elgin's governorship in Canada (1846-1854) was a time of serious political and economic crisis. Elgin's successful negotiation of the difficulties confronting his administration

constitutes an important turning point in the history of
Canada. The personalities of James Bruce, eighth Earl
of Elgin, and of Henry George, third Earl Grey, the
Colonial Secretary from 1846 to 1852, are of great significance in their bearing on the events of the period. The
Elgin-Grey Papers, the private correspondence which
passed between the two, indicate how closely they co-
operated. (*See Reading No. 7.*) Grey, who was dogmatic,
tenacious of his views, and prone to pompous lectures,
had certain ideas which he advanced courageously. He
believed in responsible government and free trade and
desired to reduce British expenditures on the colonies and
to utilize the sale of crown lands to facilitate emigration
to the colonies. Elgin, a man of liberal sympathies and
opinions, had a great capacity to adjust his views in accordance with the practical possibilities of a situation.
In Canada he displayed strong moral courage and a
capacity to adhere firmly to principles in which he believed. He showed great adroitness in persuading Grey to
modify views which the Colonial Secretary sometimes
developed without due regard for Canadian conditions.
Elgin, too, believed strongly in responsible government.
Unlike Durham and Sydenham, Elgin practiced a policy
of conciliating the French and integrating them in the
Canadian political system. He was anxious also to satisfy
the Canadian desire for a reciprocity treaty with the
United States.

The working out of responsible government and the
repercussions of British policies of free trade involved
Elgin in grave difficulties. The reformers under Baldwin
and Lafontaine took office in 1848 and in 1849 introduced the Rebellion Losses Bill to compensate those who
had suffered property damage in Lower Canada during
the rebellion of 1837. Despite Tory demands for veto of
the bill, Elgin insisted on signing it. He maintained that
since the measure had passed the legislature it was a
test case in responsible government. Riotous scenes followed in Montreal. The governor-general was pelted with
refuse in the streets. The parliament buildings were burnt,
and the city was in a state of wild disorder for several
days. The sequel to this crisis occurred in the autumn.
Alienated by the bill and by the loss of protection in

Britain, the Montreal Tories demanded annexation of
Canada to the United States. The proposal received considerable support in Lower Canada, although little in the
Upper Province. Grey and Elgin refused to countenance
the annexation movement, and with the return of prosperity in 1850 orderly political conditions were re-
established. By co-operating with the Tories, who returned
to office in 1854, Elgin helped to establish the principle
that the governor-general would work cordially with his
political advisors no matter what political group they
might represent. His administration had marked the final
vindication of responsible government in Canada.

French Canada. The formation of the Reform
Party in the 1840's and the achievement of responsible
government accomplished an important turning point in
the development of French Canada. Since the conquest,
the French Canadians had been unalterably determined
to preserve "our laws, our language, our religion"; the
struggle for *survivance* was one of the great themes of
post-conquest Canadian history. There were two proposed
methods of achieving *survivance:* (1) by co-operation
with Anglo-Saxons of goodwill, some from outside Quebec and (2) by development of the French in isolation
as a separate fearful parochial group. The rebellion of
1837 was in effect the result of an attempt to apply the
second policy. Moreover, in the years immediately following the rebellion, the French were sullen and suspicious of Anglo-Saxons and were disposed to live to
themselves.

The decision of Lafontaine to co-operate with Baldwin
and the Anglo-Saxon reformers was of decisive importance in arresting the isolationist trend. The Baldwin-
Lafontaine combination was one of the great Anglo-
French alliances of Canadian political history. In spite of
the opposition of Papineau, Lafontaine was able to carry
a large section of his compatriots into the Reform Party.
From this time on in Canadian History there was always
a considerable number of French politicians willing to
co-operate with Anglo-Saxons, although separation, too,
continued to have its advocates.

The Extension of Responsible Government. The
concession of responsible government left some controls

in the hands of the British government, and the process of fully emerging from British tutelage occupied the next hundred years. Some extensions of the principle occurred shortly after 1849. In 1850, Francis Hincks initiated the struggle to secure for Canada the right to issue its own coinage. The campaign was brought to a successful conclusion by William Cayley (1807-1890), as Canadian minister of finance, and the new decimal coins were issued in Canada, in the summer of 1858. In 1859, A. T. Galt (1817-1893), Cayley's successor, engaged in a famous exchange with the Duke of Newcastle. (*See Reading No. 8.*) Galt vindicated the right of Canada to control its own tariff policy. In 1860-1861, he secured recognition by the British government of the right of the British North American colonies to grant each other preferences which discriminated against other countries including other portions of the Empire.

Relations with the United States 1783-1860. Relations with the United States were characterized by gradual extension of trade, but also by a series of controversies which accentuated the Loyalist tradition of anti-Americanism. High diplomacy in regard to British North America was still in the hands of the British, who, according to a common Canadian opinion, sadly bungled it. Many of the outstanding issues between the colonies and the United States were results of the Treaty of Versailles of 1783. It had left the boundary settlement and the rights of Americans in the Atlantic fisheries far from clear. Controversies over the boundary between the United States and the colonies were settled by the Convention of 1818, the Webster-Ashburton Treaty of 1842, and the Oregon Treaty of 1846. Disputes over the question of the rights of American fishermen in the coastal waters of the British North American colonies continued through the period and produced a sharp controversy in the early 1850's. The principal issue was whether the three-mile line should be drawn in such a way as to admit American fishing vessels to the bays and inlets along the coast of the colonies.

Meanwhile, increasingly close trade relations between Canada and the United States led to an agitation in the late 1840's for a reciprocity agreement giving free access to American markets for the principal Canadian exports. The campaign for reciprocity was begun in 1846 by a Canadian, W. H. Merritt (1793-1862) and later taken up by British diplomats. Development of the fisheries controversy ·in 1852 enhanced the prospects of a reciprocity agreement. By 1854 the British Government, which was on the eve of the Crimean War, was anxious to secure a settlement of the fisheries and reciprocity questions. The Pierce administration in the United States also wished to settle these issues. Lord Elgin, who negotiated the treaty in June 1854, conciliated southern American opponents of the measure with great skill; it was ratified in Congress in August, partly as a result of the efforts of a professional lobbyist named I. D. Andrews. The treaty included the four Maritime Colonies as well as Canada. It admitted into the United States and the colonies free of duty a list of natural products which included grain, flour, and breadstuffs; animals; fresh, smoked, and salted meats; fish of all kinds; timber and lumber. All the principal exports of the colonies were in the list. The treaty provided for reciprocal free access to the coastal fisheries, with reservations protecting the salmon, shad, and shellfish industries. United States vessels were admitted to the navigation of the St. Lawrence and the Canadian canals. The treaty began a period of closer economic relations between the colonies, particularly Canada, and the United States. During its operation (1854-1866), there was a considerable increase in trade between the British North American colonies and the United States. However, a number of other factors, such as the industrial and railway boom in the United States and Canada in the 1850's and the Crimean and American Civil Wars, helped to produce this result.

Economic Development 1790-1867. During this period eastern Canada's loss of control over the fur trade was balanced by the emergence of new staple trades: timber, lumber, and wheat and by the beginnings of industrial development in Upper and Lower Canada. The export trade to Great Britain and the United States was extended. These developments were facilitated by the construction of canals and railways.

The absorption of the North West Company by the

Hudson's Bay Company in 1821 ended Montreal's participation in the fur trade; but already, as a result of
British preference during the Napoleonic Wars, the export trade in square timber to Great Britain had reached
important proportions. William Price began to exploit
the Saguenay country about 1825. The opening up of
Upper Canada resulted in the increased production of
wheat and flour. By 1867 staple products (wheat, timber,
lumber, and fish) were still the basis of the Canadian
economy; but there had been a considerable expansion
of Upper Canadian manufactures in the 1850's and
1860's. Factories established in Toronto, Hamilton, along
the north shore of Lake Ontario, and in what is now
southwestern Ontario, involved considerable increase in
flour-milling, brewing and distilling, woolen and cotton
industries. Agricultural implement factories were established by Daniel Massey in 1847 and by Alanson Harris
in 1857. Economic expansion was accompanied by the
establishment of banks and other financial institutions,
including the Bank of Montreal in 1817; the Bank of
Upper Canada in 1822; the Bank of Toronto and the
Toronto Stock Exchange in 1855. The Canadian Bank of
Commerce was established in 1867.

The construction of canals and railways was calculated
partly to develop Canada itself, and partly to enable the
merchants, especially those in Montreal, to capture the
through traffic between the American middle west and
Europe. The expansionist process derived great impetus
from the enthusiastic advocacy of such men as W. H.
Merritt and Thomas C. Keefer (1821-1915). The Welland
Canal was completed in 1829; the Rideau, in 1834 and
the St. Lawrence Canals, in 1848. Slight beginnings in
railroad construction were made in the 1830's and 1840's;
but the great railway boom came to British North
America in the decade of the fifties. Some two thousand
miles of track were laid down. The most important line
was the Grand Trunk Railway, which, by 1860, connected
Detroit, Sarnia, Quebec, and Portland, Maine. The line
was promoted and built by the British contracting Company, Peto, Brassey, Jackson, and Betts and by Canadian
interests including A. T. Galt, D. L. Macpherson (1818-
1896), and Casimer Gzowski (1813-1898). They secured

extensive assistance from the Canadian government. The
Great Western Railway was promoted by a Hamilton
group which included Sir Allan MacNab (1798-1862)
and Isaac Buchanan (1810-1883). By 1860 the company
had completed lines connecting Windsor, Sarnia, Hamilton, Niagara Falls, and Toronto. Transportation which
had been characterized by such difficulties as those described in *Reading No. 9* was revolutionized by the
coming of the railways. They were of prime importance
in the development of the country, but failed to capture
much of the through trade between the American middle
west and Europe.

    Religion in the Colonies 1760-1867. The Roman
Catholic Church, already firmly established in Lower
Canada, held its ground there and became established in
Upper Canada, chiefly as a result of immigration of the
Glengarry Scots and subsequently the Irish. It became
established also in the Maritimes, particularly Cape
Breton, which was mainly settled by Highland Scots.
Early progress of the Church of England in the Maritimes
resulted from the arrival of British garrisons and United
Empire Loyalists. The first bishop of Nova Scotia, Charles
Inglis (1734-1816), was consecrated in 1787. Expansion
of the Church of England in Canada may be traced in
the numbers of its clergy. Jacob Mountain, the first bishop
of Quebec (1749-1825), began his career in 1793 with
nine clergy under his jurisdiction; by the death of the
second bishop of Quebec, Charles James Stewart (1775-
1837), the number had risen to eighty-five. Under the
third bishop of Quebec, G. J. Mountain (1789-1863), the
Diocese of Quebec was divided into five dioceses (Quebec, Montreal, Toronto, Huron, and Ontario) with a total
of nearly four hundred clergy. (*See Reading No. 10.*)
Presbyterianism entered Upper Canada from the United
States by way of the Niagara River, but after 1840 Scottish and Irish immigration altered its tone and re-established connections with Great Britain. In the Maritimes
and in the fur-traders' church, the St. Gabriel Street
congregation in Montreal, Presbyterianism was British in
origin. The Free Church secession in Scotland in 1843
produced a similar division in the Canadian church.
American Methodists came into Canada by way of the

Bay of Quinte, and until 1824 Canada was part of the New York Conference, which was later called the Genesee Conference. The Canada Conference was set up in 1824 and four years later became an independent Canadian church.

Meanwhile, the British Wesleyans had come in and established charges between Montreal and Kingston. The union of the Canadian and Wesleyan churches was engineered by Egerton Ryerson in 1833; they divided in 1840 but were reunited in 1847. This early union was a first step toward the establishment of the Methodist Church of Canada which was formed by the union of central Canadian and Maritime Methodists in 1874. The strength of the Baptist Church in Nova Scotia reflected the pre-Loyalist New England origins of many of its people. The Newlight revival, in which Henry Alline (1748-1784) was the moving force, largely destroyed the Congregational Church in Nova Scotia and diverted many of its adherents to the Baptist Church.

Even more worthy of attention than the institutional development of the churches is the record of their ideas. Despite grave differences, they shared a common body of Christian belief. All believed that man was a sinner, bound for hell, unable to rescue himself, in need of a redeemer, but capable of salvation if he would avail himself of the divine sacrifice on his behalf. All accepted the authority of a Bible which all believed to be divinely inspired. All regarded the achievement of everlasting life as the dominant aim of the Christian. His own material, earthly comfort, while pleasant, was of secondary importance. The differences between the churches were frequently more apparent than this area of general agreement. The Romans and High Anglicans had special ideas about the historic role of the church and the clergy; they stressed the importance of membership in the corporate church and participation in its sacraments. They differed in their attitude toward Biblical interpretation and toward the papacy. The adherents of the Reformed Faith (Low Church Anglicans and Presbyterians) emphasized the distinction between the visible and invisible churches, the role of justification by faith in the process of salvation and the sovereignty of God. They also laid tremendous emphasis upon the study of the Bible and the place of knowledge in the process of salvation. The Pietists (Methodists and Quakers) agreed with the Reformed Church in regard to the invisible church and justification by faith, but stressed the role of free will in the process of salvation. Their distinctive feature was stress upon the "Inner Light," as distinct from any external agency in the Christian's achievement of salvation.

Social Development. Canadian life in the nineteenth century was characterized by the arduous, rural existence of settlers establishing their farms in frontier areas and by the pleasanter provincial society of such urban centres as Quebec, Montreal, and Toronto. Life on the frontier was vividly and feelingly described by such pioneer women as Susannah Moodie (1803-1885) and her sister, Catherine Parr Traill (1802-1899). (*See Reading No. 11.*) It was a lonely existence for the women and a life of very hard work with few diversions for both men and women. Frontiersmen developed qualities of independence, but they also depended upon each other for such services as barn-raisings and threshings. Educational and medical facilities were scant. National groups, such as the Highlanders in the Kildonan area near London, tended at first to be segregated; but E. A. Talbot (1801-1839), a settler in the London area, and Mrs. Moodie both commented on the tendency of all to assume a common North American culture of manners, customs, and habits of life. Many of the settlers had large families; the author has the record of a typical Anglo-Saxon family in the Fordyce area in Quebec which had thirteen children between 1806 and 1830. The frontier was a time of testing. There was much drinking and gambling; many settlers went to pieces and lost everything. Many others endured and developed qualities of native toughness.

Urban society in centres like Quebec was similar to that of English provincial towns in the period. Kate Mountain (1830-1886), Amelia Murray, Frances Monck, and the English journalist, W. H. Russell, have described the life of polite society in Quebec: its riding, formal dinners and balls, and its musical evenings. (*See Reading No. 12.*) Until the withdrawal of the British garrison in 1871, British officers were much in demand; the "Quebec boys," according to one observer, were "looked down upon" by the local young ladies. Life in Toronto was similar. Here the tone was set by the older Family Compact families: the Boultons, the Robinsons, the Baldwins, and by newer arrivals: the Gooderhams, the Wortses, William McMaster (1811-1877), and William Davies (1831-1921). Not all was comfort in the cities, especially among the poorer elements. Mrs. G. J. Mountain, the bishop's wife, commented on the fact that many poor people in Quebec never had the services of a doctor since they were unable to afford it. People in the towns were more subject to epidemics like the cholera epidemics of 1832, 1847, and 1849.

Culture in the Colonies. There was some indication of a native Canadian culture prior to 1867. It is true that it was largely derivative, imported from Great Britain and the United States, but there were signs of a native Canadian strain both as to themes and viewpoint.

In the Maritimes in the pre-Revolutionary period, Puritans from New England wrote hymns, diaries, sermons, and controversial treatises. Henry Alline, the Evangelist, is an example. Jacob Bailey (1731-1808) and Jonathan Odell (1737-1818) produced a quite voluminous literature, largely polemical and descriptive of their experiences during, and after, the Revolution. The best-known Maritime writer was T. C. Haliburton (1796-1865), the creator of Sam Slick. Sam was a Yankee clockmaker and peddler who travelled around New England and the Maritime colonies.

Writing in the Canadas included books on history and politics. The best known were those of Robert Christie (1788-1856) and Alpheus Todd (1821-1884). Mrs. Jameson (1794-1860), Mrs. Moodie, and Mrs. Traill wrote memoirs describing life on the frontier. John Richardson (1706-1852) wrote historical novels. The most important poets were Charles Sangster (1822-1893) and Charles Heavysege (1816-1876), the author of two dramatic poems, *Saul* and *Jephthah's Daughter*. A number of periodicals, most of them shortlived, were established during the period. Of these the most successful was the *Literary Garland* (1838-1851), a monthly magazine which was published in Montreal. The newspapers of the period served chiefly to express the political opinions of their proprietors. They were powerful instruments in the formation of public opinion. Notable examples were the *Nova Scotian,* published in Halifax by Joseph Howe, William Lyon Mackenzie's *Colonial Advocate,* and George Brown's (1818-1880) Toronto *Globe.*

Theatres flourished in Quebec and Halifax in the eighteenth century and often showed first string British plays a few weeks after their production in London. The principal Toronto theatre, the *Royal Lyceum,* opened in 1848. Casts in its plays included both amateurs and professionals. Its plays were mainly British, but *Uncle Tom's Cabin* was produced in 1858. Amateur theatricals were a pleasant diversion for officers of British garrisons and often produced much hilarity.

Music in the Canadian cities was mainly vocal, much of it associated with the churches. The Philharmonic Society was organized in Toronto in 1846. In 1851 the Toronto Vocal and Musical Society was formed by Dr. J. P. Clarke. Many people, like the Mountains in Quebec, had musical evenings when instrumental numbers, vocal solos, and duets were performed. A favourite form of musical entertainment in Toronto was the concert. It gave scope for individual amateurs, both vocalists and instrumentalists.

Other forms of entertainment flourished during the period. Circuses had appeared by 1866, when an American company advertized in Toronto its "Grand Combination Circus and Trained Animals." The more well-to-do Canadians in the urban centres danced the fashionable dances of the period, the quadrille and the polka. Humbler people too had their music and dancing. Kate Mountain's description of the wedding of one of the maids employed by her family gives a vivid picture of social life among the servants. (*See Reading No. 13.*) Winter sports were popular, and the rink at Quebec was an important centre for the social élite, both native Canadians and also officers from the garrison.

There was an efflorescence of French literary culture during the middle of the nineteenth century. Among its leading personalities were François-Xavier Garneau (1809-1866), the historian; Joseph Octave Crémazie,

(1827-1879), the bookseller and romantic poet, and Antoine Gérin-Lajoie (1824-1882), the novelist. These men sang the glories of Quebec. Their writings represented a conscious effort to prove Durham and other critics wrong in their depreciation of French culture.

Education. The unchallenged supremacy of Christian belief in Canada created the problem of whether education should be in the hands of the state or the churches. The colonies had decided by 1850 that primary and secondary education should be in the hands of the state; but many problems in regard to the place of Christianity in the system were still to be answered. The basis for the Ontario system was laid by acts passed by the legislature of the Province of Canada in 1846 and 1847 on the recommendation of Egerton Ryerson, the Superintendent of Education for Upper Canada. The system was essentially Christian in basic philosophy, but emphatically nonsectarian. Ryerson insisted that it was possible to teach Christian truth and morality without sectarian dogma. The system was a good practical one with few of the extras of later days. The courses consisted almost entirely of English, mathematics, geography, and history with some attention to religious knowledge. Roman Catholics were permitted to establish separate schools which were given a measure of state support. In 1846 the Canadian legislature laid the basis for the Lower Canadian system of primary and secondary education. Roman Catholic and Protestant schools held the field side by side as, in effect, two systems of separate schools.

Public schools made varying degrees of progress in the Maritime colonies. The Nova Scotian system really began in 1811 with legislation in regard to schools which laid the basis for common schools. William Dawson (1820-1899), later the principal of McGill University, was appointed the first Superintendent of Education in Nova Scotia in 1850. New Brunswick, which had five hundred schools by 1844-1845, appointed its first Superintendent of Education in 1852. The establishment of common schools in Prince Edward Island dated from the first Education Act which was passed in 1852. In the Northwest, education began under religious auspices. By 1844 the Church of England had nine schools in the Red River area, including the one established by the Rev. John West (1775-1845) shortly after his arrival in 1820.

In the field of higher education where the denominational colleges: Victoria at Cobourg, Trinity in Toronto, Queen's at Kingston, Bishop's at Lennoxville, Mount Allison at Sackville, Acadia at Wolfville, St. Francis Xavier at Antigonish, and King's at Windsor, Nova Scotia. They held the field side by side with the secularized institutions, the University of Toronto, McGill, Dalhousie, and, after 1860, the University of New Brunswick. The establishment of University College as part of the University of Toronto in 1853 was an important step in the direction of nonsectarian liberal education. Like other arts colleges of the period, University College had a dominantly humanistic curriculum, although it gradually made concessions to science. Typical of the courses offered in Anglican colleges was that offered by Bishop's College, which included Classical and English literature and composition, history, mathematics, natural and experimental philosophy, chemistry, logic, rhetoric, moral philosophy, Hebrew, and divinity.

The Maritime Colonies (1783-1867). For the Maritimes, the period between 1783 and 1867 was one of development and of almost general prosperity. Each of the three colonies (Nova Scotia, New Brunswick, and Prince Edward Island) had its own special problems. The politics of Nova Scotia was for a long time plagued by the struggle between the dominant oligarchy at Halifax and the Assembly, which asserted its right to control the casual and territorial revenues of the colony. The oligarchy controlled the Council. In New Brunswick there was a similar struggle between the Council and the Assembly, chiefly over the control of finance and education. Those quarrels largely disappeared with the concession of responsible government in the 1840's. In Prince Edward Island the principal problem was the struggle between the colonists and absentee landowners until passage of the Land Purchase Act of 1875, which made provision for the purchase of land by the tenants.

Trade in the Maritimes was stimulated by the Napoleonic Wars and later, by the Reciprocity Treaty of 1854 and the American Civil War. The principal Maritime industries were the fisheries, lumbering, the building of wooden ships, and to a lesser extent, the coal and agricultural industries. In the economy of the British Empire after the American Revolution, the Maritimes were expected to perform the functions performed by New England in the old empire. They were to be a centre of shipping and shipbuilding, a base for the North Atlantic fisheries, and a source of provisions and lumber for Newfoundland and the West Indies. While not fulfilling this role completely, the Maritimes enjoyed a satisfactory level of prosperity.

Newfoundland's development was somewhat different. For a long time the British government discouraged development of Newfoundland as a colony, in the attempt to benefit the west coast fishing industry of England. They abandoned this policy at the end of the eighteenth century, and from that time on, the fishing industry was carried on mainly by resident Newfoundland fishermen. Newfoundland was officially recognized as a colony in 1824 and given representative government in 1832.

The Northwest. British control of the region west of the Great Lakes came as a result of the westward penetration of the fur traders. Building on the achievements of the French, the Hudson's Bay Company and the North West Company carved out a vast western empire in the late eighteenth and early nineteenth centuries. Much of northern Canada and the Pacific coastal region was explored by the Nor'westers Alexander Mackenzie (1763-1820), Simon Fraser (1776?-1862), and David Thompson (1770-1857) and by Samuel Hearne (1745-1792) of the Hudson's Bay Company. Both companies maintained networks of trading posts in the west. After absorption of the North West Company in 1821, the whole of what is now the continental part of western Canada was under the control of the Hudson's Bay Company.

The first important settlement in the Northwest was the Red River Colony. It was established in 1811 by Scottish settlers who had been sent by Thomas Douglas, fifth Earl of Selkirk (1771-1820). The Selkirk settlers founded their colony near the junction of the Red and

Assiniboine Rivers, on land ceded by the Hudson's Bay
Company. The settlement experienced early difficulties:
armed opposition from the Nor'westers, plagues of
locusts, and a disastrous flood in 1826. Having survived
these early tribulations, the settlement experienced a
modest prosperity. It remained under the control of the
Hudson's Bay Company until 1869. In the 1850's and
1860's, settlers from Canada led by Dr. John Schultz
(1840-1896) began an agitation for the overthrow of
company rule and for union with Canada. Union was also
advocated in Canada, particularly by George Brown and
the Toronto *Globe*.

Fur-trading activity in the Pacific coastal region was
begun by the Nor'westers in 1806 and continued by the
Hudson's Bay Company after 1821. Heavy American
immigration into Oregon in the 1840's made it seem likely
that the Americans would occupy the coast up to the
Russian holdings on the line 54-40. The British government was able to preserve the position of the Hudson's
Bay Company by negotiation of the Oregon Treaty in
1846. It established the northern American boundary
along the forty-ninth parallel. After the signing of the
treaty, the Company established its principal Pacific base
at Fort Victoria on Vancouver Island and shifted its
principal fur-trading activities to the Fraser and the
Thompson Rivers. Vancouver Island was ceded to the
Hudson Bay Company in 1849, and James Douglas
(1803-1877), the chief factor of the company, became
the second governor of the new colony in 1851. Douglas,
the strong man of early British Columbian history, was
able by his initiative and determination to prevent the
domination of the mainland by the United States. After
the discovery of gold on the Fraser and the consequent
influx of settlers, he made himself the *de facto* governor
of the mainland, prevented disorder, and was subsequently appointed governor of the new colony of British
Columbia in 1858. He also continued as the governor of
Vancouver Island, which was repurchased from the company. Vancouver Island had been granted a legislative
assembly in 1856. In 1864 the mainland colony was given
a legislative council which included appointed officials

and elected representatives. In 1866 both colonies were brought under one government. The decline of the boom after 1865 left British Columbia with a heavy debt and in desperate need of capital, immigrants, and markets. In 1867 it was still uncertain whether British Columbia's eventual destiny lay in independence, union with Canada, or annexation to the United States.

Politics in Canada 1849-1864. After 1849 the old Reform Party in the Province of Canada disintegrated, and the result was an important re-alignment of political groups. Prior to 1849 the desire for responsible government had held the Reform Party together. It had consisted of French *Bleus* and *Rouges* and Upper Canadian moderate reformers and radicals, the last group both urban and rural. The reformers had been opposed by the Family Compact Tories and the Moderate Conservatives from Upper Canada, and by the English-speaking Conservatives from Lower Canada. After the achievement of responsible government, differences developed in the Reform Party. This made possible the formation of the Liberal-Conservative administration of 1854, mainly through the organizing genius of John A. Macdonald (1815-1891); it consisted of the three English-speaking Conservative groups and also the Quebec *Bleus*. Some former supporters of Francis Hincks also joined the alliance.

The English-speaking Conservatives displayed much the same attitudes which have already been noted in reference to Family Compact Toryism; but there was a new emphasis upon Canadian autonomy, particularly after the achievement of responsible government. Conservatives played their part in the establishment of the decimal currency, and it was a Conservative, A. T. Galt, who vindicated Canada's right to control its own tariff policy. The English-speaking Conservatives were strong advocates of canals and railways. These economic policies were indicative of the fact that Canadian Conservatism was essentially the party of business. The party tended to adopt the policies which businessmen required. The French *Bleus* were different. They were chiefly concerned with the defence of "our laws, our language, our religion" and with obtaining patronage for French Canadians. They regarded membership in the Conservative Party as the best means to secure their objectives.

The new Reform alliance consisted of Quebec *Rouges,* Upper Canadian radicals or Clear Grits, and moderate reformers. The Clear Grits represented an agrarian and democratic trend in the Reform Party. They favoured universal suffrage, vote by ballot, and the application of the elective principle to the office of governor. These were suggestive of Jacksonian democracy and contemporary English radicalism. The Clear Grits were anti-clerical and strongly Orange in opinion. The *Rouges* shared the ideas of the Clear Grits in regard to democratic reform. They were distinctly anti-clerical, a grave handicap in electoral contests in Lower Canada. The moderate reformers derived their ideas from constitutional reformers such as Robert Baldwin and also from British middle-class liberalism. George Brown (1818-1880) of Toronto, the principal advocate of moderate reform, emphasized laissez-faire business enterprise and political constitutionalism. Mainly as a result of Brown's vigorous advocacy of representation by population, the Reform Party made considerable gains in Upper Canada. From 1858 to 1864 the two parties were so equally balanced as to threaten the province of Canada as a whole, with political deadlock.

Confederation. Confederation in 1867 was one of the great landmarks in Canadian history. Although the union at first included only four provinces, they were the nucleus to which the others were eventually added. Confederation had been discussed by a number of people, notably by Durham and Elgin, and in 1858 by A. T. Galt. In the 1860's a series of factors developed which were destined to bring about the success of the movement. Of prime importance was the political deadlock in Canada in 1864. It forced the two parties, Conservative and Reform, to form a coalition government pledged to bring about confederation. Other important factors were the fear of political or economic aggression from the United States during a period of strained relations resulting from the American Civil War; the need for an alternative commercial policy after the abrogation of the

Reciprocity Treaty in 1865-1866; and the desire to secure control of the Northwest territories and to build a railway to the Pacific and another linking the Province of Canada with the Maritimes. The Canadians and the other colonists were anxious to remain within the Empire and felt that they would have a better chance of doing so as part of a United Canada. Not the least of the motives inspiring the fathers of confederation was the vision of a "dominion from sea to sea" and a wider political field in which to exercise their talents. (*See Reading No. 14.*)

The movement toward confederation makes exciting reading from the preliminary conference at Charlottetown in September, 1864, to the passage of the British North America Act in March 1867, and its promulgation on July 1, 1867. To some extent the B.N.A. Act provided Canada with a written constitution (*See Reading No. 15*), although its working depended upon many precedents and statutes which Canada inherited from the British political tradition. The principle of responsible government was carried over into the new political system. The Act established representative parliamentary institutions in the dominion government and in that of the provinces. The distribution of powers between provinces and dominion was indicated particularly in sections 91, 92, and 93. The dominion was given the right to legislate for the peace, order, and good government of the dominion; this section included twenty-nine specifically mentioned powers. The provinces were given seventeen assigned powers including property and civil rights, and education. By section 133 the French language was given equal status with English in the parliament at Ottawa, the federal law courts, and the Quebec legislature.

— 4 —

YOUNG DOMINION, 1867-1914

The Rounding Out of Confederation. Canada
made important progress toward nation building after
1867 by extending the area of the dominion, developing
a sound and coherent economy, and by gradually producing a distinctive Canadian culture.

The territorial area of the dominion was rapidly extended after 1867. The first acquisition was the territory
previously controlled by the Hudson's Bay Company and
known officially as Rupert's Land and the Northwest
Territory. Its entry into confederation was delayed by
the Red River insurrection of 1869-1870. The insurrection was a protest movement by the Métis, French-
Indian half-breeds, who were alarmed at the prospect of
Canadian domination. It was led by the clever but un-
balanced Louis Riel (1844-1885) and was largely inspired
by a Roman Catholic priest, Father Ritchot. Riel and the
Métis rose on November 2, 1869 and seized Fort Garry.
In December, 1869, he established a provisional government. This eventually collapsed in August, 1870, when Red
River was occupied by British and Canadian troops. The
legislation providing for the establishment of Red River
as the Province of Manitoba was passed by the Canadian
Parliament and received the royal signature on May 12,
1870. Canada secured official possession of the Red River
settlement on July 15, 1870 when Rupert's Land and the
Northwest Territory was transferred by the British Government to the dominion. The Canadian act of May 12,
1870 was confirmed by a British statute, the British North
America Act of 1871 (34 and 35 Victoria, chap. 28).
British Columbia entered the dominion in 1871 on condition that a transcontinental railway should be started

46

in three years and completed in ten. Prince Edward Island was embarrassed by debts mainly incurred in railroad construction. The colony entered the union in 1873 when offered "better terms" by Macdonald.

Meanwhile, the Canadian government was devising the policies designed to develop a coherent and durable economic system. An important part of the grand strategy was the policy of tariff protection that was undertaken to foster native industry, particularly after the development of Sir John Macdonald's national policy in the late 1870's. Financial machinery, intended to facilitate economic expansion, was another phase of the process. After an initial struggle between Toronto and Montreal banking interests in 1869-1871 over the nature of the system, bank acts were passed by Sir Francis Hincks in 1870 and 1871 (33 Victoria, chap. 2 and 34 Victoria, chap. 5) which made possible the expansion of the banks in both cities. Railway construction in the period was of vital importance to Canada. The Intercolonial Railroad connecting central Canada with the Maritime Provinces was completed in 1876. Efforts to build a transcontinental railway to British Columbia encountered grave obstacles. The first Canadian Pacific Railway Company collapsed after the disclosure of the fact that its president, Sir Hugh Allan (1810-1882), had given extensive financial assistance to the Conservatives in the election of 1872. The second company was chartered in 1880, under the presidency of George Stephen (1829-1921), a Montreal railway promoter and textile manufacturer. This company was more fortunate. After great difficulties in the financing and construction of the railroad, Stephen and his colleagues, Donald Smith (later Lord Strathcona, 1820-1914) and William Van Horne (1843-1915), completed the line to Vancouver in November, 1885.

Rise of the Cities. While the national economic policy was being worked out, Montreal and Toronto were emerging as the great Canadian metropolises. They were examples of the process described by N. S. B. Gras (*An Introduction to Economic History,* 1922), by which a metropolis achieves and retains "dominance" over a dependent area or hinterland. The metropolis, said Gras, becomes, "the focus of local trade and the centre through

which normal economic relations with the outside world
are maintained." In its progress toward metropolitan
status, the city passes through four stages: organization
of the market, development of manufactures either in
the city itself or in its immediate hinterland, construction
of a transportation network, and the development of a
mature financial organization to mobilize capital and
facilitate its employment. During the latter half of the
nineteenth century, Montreal and Toronto proceeded far
towards metropolitan status.

Montreal, which had a population of 130,000 in 1871
and 254,000 in 1891, was larger, wealthier, and more
powerful than Toronto in this period. The rise of Montreal was the result of such factors as the trade in furs,
timber, and wheat; the construction of the Welland, St.
Lawrence, and Chambly Canals and of railways, particularly the Grand Trunk. Also of importance was the
improvement of port facilities and the development of
ocean navigation. Many able citizens, including the
Molsons, the Redpaths, George Stephen, and Donald
Smith, gave leadership in this process of development.
The Bank of Montreal was the country's principal bank.
The Canadian Pacific Railway, built by a Montreal company between 1880-1855 had its head office in the city.

By the second half of the century, Toronto was providing serious competition for Montreal. Toronto enjoyed
important geographic advantages, including the possession
of a good port. Its initial development was the result of
its choice by Lieutenant-Governor John Graves Simcoe
(1752-1806) as the capital of Upper Canada in 1793. Its
rise in the nineteenth century was largely a result of
the vigour and enterprise of such businessmen as the
McMasters, the Wortses, the Gooderhams, and the Allans.
The city derived great advantage from tariff protection-
ism, which tended to develop local industry. The population of Toronto was 30,000 in 1851; 56,000 in 1871;
and 181,000 in 1891. The city which had become an
important marketing centre by 1850, achieved important
developments in manufactures in the 1850's and 1860's,
while the construction of railways, including the Grand
Trunk and the Northern, connected the city more firmly
with its hinterland. Toronto had begun to develop the

financial machinery which facilitated its expansion. In 1871, the city was successful in its struggle with Montreal over bank legislation. In 1890, the Canadian Bank of Commerce had assets of over twenty-two million dollars and was the second bank in the dominion, although far behind the Bank of Montreal, which had assets of over forty-seven million dollars. Toronto made a vigorous, but unsuccessful, attempt to secure the contract to build the transcontinental railway which the dominion government had promised to British Columbia. Montreal gained the contract, and the C. P. R. was built. By the turn of the century, the two cities had emerged as the great centres of Canadian economic development, largely controlling the country's industry, transportation and finance, and through them, Canadian agriculture.

Political Parties (1867-1896). The political parties which emerged in this period were virtual federations of regional groups which had existed prior to 1867. They were built around the parties which had been formed in the Province of Canada in the years between 1854 and 1858. The Liberal-Conservatives retained their original name; the Reformers became Liberals. In each party the Ontario and Quebec group was united with allied groups in the Maritimes and the West.

The years between 1867 and 1896 were the Golden Age of Conservatism. Except for one interlude (1873-1878), the Conservatives were in office for the whole period. They were mainly responsible for the policies of political and economic expansion which we have already noted on page 47. French Canadians supported these policies of development and in turn were supported in the defence of French culture. The Conservatives were normally keen adherents of the Empire; but their leader, Sir John Macdonald, showed considerable independence in his relations with the British, especially when Gladstone was in power. In large measure the success of the Conservatives was a result of Macdonald's leadership. The legend has grown up of the erratic, but utterly charming, political chieftain always able to "dish the Whigs"; but this judgment is unfair. D. G. Creighton's life of Macdonald (*John A. Macdonald, The Old Chieftain,* 1955) emphasizes his great gifts, essential honesty, and solid achievements. Macdonald regarded his task, especially after confederation, as "the continental task of nation building." He thought of this task in terms of a Canada great and strong, but linked by indissoluble ties to Crown and Empire. He combined with this awareness of ultimate objectives a superb ability to hold disparate elements, French and English, Roman Catholic and Protestant, Easterner and Westerner, together in one political party.

Ineffective leadership and unpopular policies doomed the Liberals to opposition for most of the period. As the commercial and agricultural party, they advocated free trade, a cautious policy of western development and gave rather ambiguous support to the policy of unrestricted reciprocity between 1887 and 1891. Under Alexander Mackenzie (1822-1892), the Liberals assumed office in 1873. They did so as a result of the Pacific Scandal: the relations of Sir Hugh Allan with the Conservatives over the C.P.R. contract. (See page 47.) The negative nature of the policy of the Liberals and the problems resulting from the depression which began in Canada in 1875 soon destroyed much of their popularity. They were soundly defeated by the Conservatives in 1878. The Liberals were responsible for one important measure, the establishment of the Supreme Court of Canada in 1875.

Breakdown of Conservatism. The last eleven years of Conservative government (1885-1896) was a period of anticlimax in which the party gradually lost its hold upon the country. The widening rift between the Orange and French Roman Catholic elements in the party was especially disastrous. Orange sentiment in Ontario had been enraged in 1870 by Louis Riel's execution of Thomas Scott, an Ontario Orangeman, during the Red River Insurrection. Riel led a second rebellion of Indians and half-breeds in Saskatchewan in 1885. After its collapse, he was convicted on a charge of high treason. There were violent demands in Ontario for his execution and equally violent demands from Quebec for pardon. He was executed on November 16, 1885. Quebec resentment of Riel's execution began the exodus of French Canadians out of the Conservative party. The French were further aggravated by Ontario protests against the Jesuit Estates

Bill of 1888. By means of this measure, Honoré Mercier (1840-1894), the Quebec Prime Minister, proposed to appropriate funds from the Jesuit estates for the use of the Roman Catholic Church, the Jesuits, and Laval University. Sir John Macdonald's refusal to challenge the bill alienated some of his Ontario supporters but did not arrest the decline of Conservative influence among the French. Federal election returns in Quebec between 1885 and 1896 indicated a continuous loss of support on the part of the Conservatives.

The Conservative decline which had begun in Quebec in the 1880's became more general in Canada in the 1890's. The death of Sir John in 1891 was a shattering blow and the party was unable to produce another leader even approaching him in stature. The economic depression of the 1890's helped to increase the unpopularity of the government. Moreover, it was embarrassed by the demands of Roman Catholics in Manitoba to re-establish the separate schools which the provincial administration under Thomas Greenway (1838-1908) had abolished. While the Conservatives declined in popularity, the Liberals were being rallied by Wilfrid Laurier (1841-1919), who had become leader in 1887. At the convention of 1893, they substantially abandoned free trade, a policy that had helped to keep them in opposition. The Conservatives were decisively defeated in the election of 1896.

Provinces vs. Dominion. During the Macdonald period, there was a determined struggle between the provinces and the dominion over their respective powers as assigned by the British North America Act. (*See Reading No. 15.*) Sir Oliver Mowat (1820-1903), the Premier of Ontario, carried a number of test cases to the Judicial Committee of the Privy Council. The decisions of the Judicial Committee revealed unexpected strength in the position of the provinces. Most of these cases were concerned with the question of the division of powers between the provinces and the dominion. Those of the federal government were contained in Section 91 of the B.N.A. Act. It declared that the dominion government could make laws for the peace, order, and good government of Canada "in relation to all matters not coming within the classes of subjects by this Act assigned exclu-

sively to the Legislatures of the Provinces." The section
listed twenty-nine specific powers which were included
in the peace, order, and good government clause but
stated that the twenty-nine did not comprise all the powers
covered by the peace, order, and good government clause.
The provinces were given sixteen specific powers including "property and civil rights." Many of the disputes arose
over the question whether certain powers come under
"peace, order, and good government" or under some provincial power, usually "property and civil rights." Test
cases were won by Ontario in connection with three provincial measures:——the Escheats and Forfeitures Act,
which had been passed in the session of 1874, the "Crooks
Act" of 1876, regulating the sale of liquor, and the Rivers
and Streams Act (1881-1884). The Judicial Committee
made it clear that the scope of provincial powers was to
be wider than Macdonald, Galt, and other fathers of
confederation had anticipated. A very important decision
was announced in 1896 in the Local Prohibition Case.
Lord Watson, of the Judicial Committee, said that the
dominion government could not "trench upon" provincial
rights in legislating under the "peace, order, and good
government" clause. In the special circumstance of a
crisis, the Judicial Committee would place a broader
interpretation on the powers of the dominion. This statement of principle was significant because of the Judicial
Committee's tendency to place disputed powers under
"property and civil rights."

Another cause of dispute was the power of the dominion government to disallow provincial legislation.
Between 1867 and 1893 Conservative governments at
Ottawa acted upon the assumption that they could disallow provincial acts on the ground that they were unjust
or oppressive, although otherwise within the competence
of the provinces. Under the Liberals who took office in
1896, this policy was abandoned. Sir Oliver Mowat, the
new Minister of Justice, declared in 1897 that it was not
his business to disallow provincial acts on grounds of injustice. His successor, Sir Allan Aylesworth (1854-1952),
followed the same policy.

The Laurier Regime 1896-1911. This period was
characterized by extensive and rapid expansion in Can-

ada, particularly in the West. Nearly two million settlers arrived in the country. In the first decade of the twentieth century there was a tremendous expansion of the wheat industry, which came to occupy a place in the Canadian economy comparable to that of furs in the French period. It was the beginning of a thirty-year period during which wheat played the dominant role in the Canadian economy. Expansion of wheat production was accompanied by remarkable industrial development. W. T. Easterbrook and H. G. J. Aitken make this clear in their volume, *Canadian Economic History*. Between 1901 and 1911 the net value of manufacturing production increased more than two and a half times; textile production more than doubled; iron and steel production more than tripled, and flour and gristmill production rose more than five-fold. The trade-union movement which had become well started in the last quarter of the nineteenth century continued to progress. The Trades and Labour Congress of Canada had been organized in 1886; it included 1,078 locals in 1902 and 1,883 locals in 1912. The organization of French-Canadian unions led to the establishment of the Canadian and Catholic Confederation of Labour in 1902.

Canadian expansion was the result of a combination of factors. Prices rose steadily in world markets during the years between 1896 and 1914. Frederick Jackson Turner's book, *The Frontier in American History,* has shown that the United States frontier as a continuous line of unsettled land could no longer be said to exist in 1890. This reduction in the supply of free land helped to divert a stream of European and American immigrants to Canada. There were also heavy capital imports into the dominion before 1914, particularly from Great Britain; two-thirds of the foreign capital held in Canada in 1914 was British. American technology, including the chilled-steel plough, the self-binding reaper, and the endless belt elevator, made an important contribution to Canadian development. The Liberals were fortunate in taking office at a time of returning prosperity, but they showed initiative and vigour in taking advantage of a happy combination of circumstances.

Sir Wilfrid Laurier, the Prime Minister, was a courtly and able man who did much to provide the Liberals with a basic philosophy. He insisted that Canadian Liberalism was in the British tradition and therefore devoid of the anti-clericalism of continental liberalism. He was not hostile to the Roman Catholic Church but asserted that the clergy must exercise restraint in their political activities. (*See Reading No. 16.*) Laurier's administration had a fine record of constructive achievement. Soon after his assumption of office, he devised a compromise settlement to the Manitoba School Question which had plagued his Conservative predecessors. The compromise permitted some religious instruction but did not re-establish separate schools. Laurier's administration developed a tariff policy that kept duties at the same general level while giving some preference to Great Britain. A notable feature of Liberal policy was the vigorous promotion of immigration by Sir Clifford Sifton (1861-1929), the Minister of the Interior. Construction of two transcontinental railways, the Grand Trunk Pacific and the Canadian Northern, was carried far toward completion. The Provinces of Alberta and Saskatchewan were established in 1905. Laurier did much to develop a nationalist viewpoint in Canadian foreign policy. He was opposed to commitments likely to involve Canada in British wars. He did accept limited Canadian participation in the South African War in order to satisfy the Anglo-Saxon wing of the party and the country. He disliked plans for centralization of the machinery of empire and was particularly cool to the proposals put forward by Sir Joseph Ward, the Prime Minister of New Zealand, at the Imperial Conference of 1911.

Quebec Nationalism 1885-1911. The section on the *Breakdown of Conservatism* has shown the extent to which Laurier and the Liberals benefited from the revival of French-Canadian nationalism after 1885. Laurier's nationalism, like Lafontaine's, favoured strong cooperation between French and English. This had been strikingly indicated by his speech at the dedication of the monument to Jacques Cartier and Brébeuf at Quebec in June, 1889. (*See Reading No. 17.*) The Riel affair, which made the fortunes of Laurier liberalism, also created Honoré Mercier in the provincial field. According to *The French Canadians 1760-1945* by Mason Wade, Mercier won the leadership of French Canada by the opening words of his speech on the Champ de Mars at Montreal, on November 22, 1885, "Riel, our brother, is dead, victim of his devotion to the cause of the Métis of whom he was the leader, victim of fanaticism and treason." Forming the Nationalist Party out of former Liberals and Conservatives, Mercier developed a very different nationalism from that of Laurier. He envisaged an embattled and isolated French group defending its culture against the Anglo-Saxon majority in Canada.

Quebec's defence of French institutions was reinforced at the turn of the century by another nationalist theme— resistance to participation in foreign wars and to the large-scale recruiting of Canadians to fight in them. The principal exponent of this idea was Henri Bourassa, a grandson of Louis Joseph Papineau. Bourassa represented the French opposition to British imperialism, which revived after 1870, and to its Canadian counterpart. The latter had shown itself in the imperialist wing of the Canada First movement which was organized in 1868 and in the establishment of branches of the Imperial Federation League between 1885 and 1888. Bourassa was a vigorous opponent of Canadian participation in the South African War. He opposed Laurier's Naval Bill of 1910, which provided for the construction of a small Canadian navy. Although he stressed the rights of French Canadians, Bourassa thought in dominion-wide terms: his isolationism was a policy which he conceived as embracing both French and English in Canada. However, he could see little prospect of Anglo-Saxon Canadians accepting his views.

Relations with the United States. After 1867, Canadian-American relations settled down to a series of negotiations in regard to commerce, the boundary, and waterways. At times the negotiations were acrimonious. To a considerable extent, they were concerned with reciprocity and the fisheries. In the discussions which culminated in the Treaty of Washington of 1871, Canada was in effect represented by Sir John Macdonald, as one of five British plenipotentiaries. Disappointed that the treaty did not contain a large measure of reciprocity, he reluctantly accepted an arrangement which opened the Canadian inshore fisheries in exchange for fish and fish oil and a cash settlement. In 1877 the cash settlement was fixed by a special commission at $5,500,000. The United States government regarded this sum as excessive but eventually paid. Before 1900 Canada made several more unsuccessful attempts to secure a reciprocity measure. A sharp controversy developed over the fisheries in 1885, when the United States abrogated the fisheries clauses of the Treaty of Washington, and the Canadian government began a vigorous policy of protecting the Atlantic fisheries against American encroachment. The dispute was settled in 1887 with the establishment of a *modus vivendi* which provided for a system of licenses for Americans fishing in Canadian coastal waters. A dispute in reference to the Alaska-British Columbia boundary was settled in 1903 by a joint British-American tribunal. The principle issue was in regard to the eastern boundary of the *lisière,* or strip along the British Columbia coast. This had been awarded to Russia in the Anglo-Russian treaty of 1825 and acquired by the United States through the Alaska purchase. The tribunal included three Americans, two Canadians, and an Englishman, Lord Alverstone. By a vote of four to two (the two Canadians) the tribunal decided in favour of the American claim. The award created much dissatisfaction in Canada. Canadians realized that the American case was strong but felt that the Canadian case had not been seriously considered at all. An important development occurred in 1909 when the British and United States governments negotiated the Boundary Waters Treaty. It established the International Joint Commission, which consisted of three American and three Canadian commissioners. The Commission has had a very good record in resolving differences and difficulties in regard to boundary waters between Canada and the United States.

The question of reciprocity was revived in 1911 when the Laurier and Taft administrations negotiated an agreement providing for a wide measure of reciprocity. The agreement was ratified by Congress but was repudiated by the Canadian people in the general election of September, 1911. In Canada, manufacturing, financial, and transportation interests opposed the measure. In addition, many Canadians feared that closer economic ties with the United States would involve Canada's secession from the Empire. In Quebec, the Conservatives were allied with French nationalists, who were less opposed to reciprocity than to Laurier's Naval Bill of 1910. The defeat of the Laurier administration in 1911 finished the question of reciprocity for over twenty years.

Religion and Philosophy 1867-1914. In the years after confederation there were significant adjustments in Protestant thought in Canada. The impact of new ideas in science and Biblical criticism began to weaken the hold of the older faith. The new ideas were chiefly British in immediate origin. The conception of man as a sinner who could only be redeemed by divine grace was partially abandoned. It was coming to be replaced by the humanist idea of man as essentially good and capable of improvement, largely through his own efforts. Two volumes were of especial importance in the development of this humanist attitude: Darwin's *Origin of Species,* which had been published in 1859, and *Essays and Reviews* (1860). In *Essays and Reviews,* a group of English scholars undertook to introduce to the British public the German critical approach to the Scriptures. Darwin's theory of evolution tended to foster a humanist conception of man. While Darwin dethroned man from the position of a special creation, he flattered human pride by establishing man as the highest of the mammals and one who had come out on top in the struggle for survival through his own adaptability. In stressing the environmental and purely human aspects of Hebrew religious development, the Biblical critics tended to supplement the humanism which Darwin had helped to foster. Both the scientists and the Biblical critics tended to destroy the orthodox conception of the Bible. The result was a growing skepticism in regard to the supernatural aspects of Christianity.

The Protestant churches in Canada were comparatively unaffected by the new ideas until about the nineties, but the universities soon felt the impact. John A. Irving, in an article in *The Canadian Historical Review,* September, 1950, has described the attempt of British Idealists like Edward Caird and T. H. Green to preserve the ethics of Christianity while discarding belief in an inspired Bible or in miraculous divine intervention. Their influence was reflected in the teaching of three men, all Scots, who were appointed to Canadian chairs of philosophy in 1871-1872: John Watson at Queen's, George Paxton Young (1819-1889) at Toronto, and John Clark Murray (1836-1917) at McGill. By 1900 such strongholds of Protestantism as Victoria College, Montreal Diocesan, and Wycliffe College had all felt the impact of the new Biblical criticism. While the faculties were still dominantly conservative, the ideas of the critics were at least being considered. Eventually in the churches, many of the clergy and laity abandoned the idea of an inspired Bible and the conception of man as a sinner saved by grace. A more optimistic estimate of human nature was largely adopted. Christianity became for many a scheme for the advocacy of social amelioration. Methodist ministers in the 1890's were influenced by the writings of Hugh Price Hughes, an English Methodist who rebuked "otherworldliness." They were influenced also by the social ideas of Dickens, George Eliot, William Morris, and others. The shift toward emphasis on the Social Gospel in Methodist preaching went much further in the twentieth century. (*See Reading No. 18.*)

Roman Catholicism in Canada was not affected so early by these humanist and critical influences. The most apparent objects of French-Canadian Roman Catholic thought were the defence of French culture in Canada and the control of liberalism within the church. Between 1858 and 1876 Bishop Bourget of Montreal (1799-1885) conducted a vigorous and eventually successful struggle against the liberal association, *Institut Canadien*. Irish, Scottish, and French Roman Catholics alike were concerned in the working out of relations between the church and the provincial governments of Manitoba and Ontario in regard to education.

Literature, Art and Criticism, 1867-1914. Canadian poetry in this period was chiefly descriptive of the Canadian landscape, although it reflected other influences also: New England transcendentalism, the romanticism of Keats, and the Irish poetry of the 1890's. Among the poets and poetesses of the period were Isabella Valancy Crawford (1850-1887), Charles G. D. Roberts (1860-1943), and Bliss Carman (1861-1929). The most important of the nature poets were Archibald Lampman (1861-1899) and Duncan Campbell Scott (1862-1947). In the first decade of the twentieth century three poets who were very different from the romantic nature school achieved prominence: W. H. Drummond (1854-1907), Robert W. Service (1874-1958) and Tom MacInnes (1867-1951). According to E. K. Brown's critical volume, *On Canadian Poetry,* the three "sought to make man the theme of their work and to show man in the raw." Drummond produced poetry in which French habitants spoke English with a characteristic French-Canadian twist. Service's best work was dramatic poetry spoken by participants in the Yukon Gold Rush of 1898. MacInnes wrote of natural man whom he regarded as bohemian. The last of the romantic naturalists, in the tradition of the early Roberts and Carman, was Marjorie Pickthall (1883-1922). Her poetry reflected the Canadian scene, but also the Bible and Irish poetry of the 1890's.

An important development in the field of literary criticism as well as political comment was the publication of a periodical, *The Week,* in Toronto between 1883 and 1896. Goldwin Smith (1823-1910), the distinguished author and journalist, exercised a decided influence over its political policy, which was anti-Orange, anti-Tory, and anti-imperialist. Its literary, dramatic, and music criticism was more mature than the naive and homely efforts which had previously passed for criticism in the Toronto papers. (*See Reading No. 19.*) The work which *The Week* had begun was carried on by *Saturday Night,* established in 1887 under the editorship of E. E. Sheppard (1855-1924). Sheppard, who remained editor until 1906, helped to encourage the development of Canadian literary talent.

Canadian artists were beginning to paint Canadian scenes. The most important painters before 1867 were Paul Kane (1810-1871) and Cornelius Krieghoff (1812-1872). Kane depicted the life of the Indians of the Northwest, and Cornelius Krieghoff painted scenes of Quebec life. Among the post-confederation painters were F. M. Bell-Smith (1846-1923), John C. Miles (d. 1911), and Paul Peel (1859-1892). In 1873 the Ontario Society of Artists began to hold annual exhibitions.

The Maritimes.   There is a tradition in the Mari-

times that they were lured into confederation by expecta-
tions which were not fulfilled. It is true that the Maritimes
did not enjoy the same expansion as that achieved by
other parts of Canada; but this was largely a result of
long-term factors such as the decline of the wooden ship.
Nor was the record all bad; by 1914 the Maritimes had
made considerable economic progress.

The economic history of the Lower Provinces in the
post-confederation period is a story of mingled gains and
reverses. After the high hopes which had been entertained
in regard to confederation, the initial period from 1867
to 1880 was disappointing. The Intercolonial Railway was
completed in 1876; but it did not bring the immense
wheat export which had been anticipated. In the decade
of the seventies, there was a substantial increase in manufacturing. The number of establishments in the Maritimes
increased by over 1,800. However, the sailing vessel,
which had figured so largely in the Martime economy, had
been ousted from the most lucrative part of the carrying
trade. During the years between 1800 and 1900, there
were far-reaching changes in the economy of the region
and a growing integration with the rest of the dominion.
Railway-building, which at first stimulated the coastal
trade, eventually cut into that of the small ports and
crippled such places as Yarmouth. There was some diversification of agriculture; the Nova Scotia apple industry was established on a long-term basis in the 1880's.
Decline in the shipbuilding industry was followed by an
increase in the export of sawn lumber. The protectionist
policies of the dominion government stimulated the iron
and steel, coal and textile industries of the Maritimes.
The Dominion Iron and Steel Company was organized in
1899. During the prewar period (1900-1914), the Maritimes were affected by general Canadian and world prosperity. They supplied world markets with lumber, fish,
potatoes, apples, and a limited range of minerals. There
was a considerable development of the iron and coal
industries. Production of Nova Scotian coal, which had
totalled 1,177,000 tons in 1880, had increased to nearly
eight million tons by 1913. Other industries, including
textiles, were expanded. Some agricultural products, notably potatoes and apples, were shipped to western Canada.

Progress toward Autonomy. During the years prior
to 1914, Canada made some progress toward autonomy,
although the gains were not as spectacular as in the period
between 1914 and 1931. The British North America Act
of 1867 gave the Dominion of Canada a wide measure
of self-government. There were, however, certain important limitations to the powers of the dominion government apart from the powers given to the provinces.
Amendment to the Canadian constitution was under the
control of the British parliament. Appeals could be made
from Canadian courts to the Judicial Committee of the
Privy Council. The treaty-making power was still a monopoly of the British government. According to the *Colonial Laws Validity Act* of 1865, Canadian legislation, if
repugnant to legislation of the British parliament, was null
and void to the extent of the repugnance. For a number
of years Canadian self-government was also limited by
the instructions and commissions issued by the imperial
parliament to the governors-general. They were ordered
to refuse assent to bills dealing with an enumerated list
of subjects. They were also instructed to exercise their
own personal judgment in the pardon of offenders condemned to death.

Canada soon improved its position with regard to two
of these limitations. In 1875, Edward Blake (1833-1912),
the Canadian Minister of Justice, persuaded the imperial
government to recast the commission and instructions to
the governors-general. They were directed to exercise the
prerogative of pardon only on ministerial advice; the
enumeration of subjects on which legislation was to be
reserved was discontinued. Some progress was made in
regard to the participation of Canadians in the negotiation of treaties. Sir John Macdonald was in effect a representative of Canada in the negotiation of the Treaty of
Washington in 1871, although officially he was merely
one of five British plenipotentiaries. Sir Charles Tupper
(1821-1915), the Canadian High Commissioner in London, was associated with Sir Robert Morier, the British
ambassador to Spain, in 1884 in an unsuccessful attempt
to negotiate a trade treaty with Spain. In 1893 Tupper and
Lord Dufferin, the British ambassador, negotiated a commercial treaty between Great Britain and France "regu-

lating the commercial relations between Canada and France in respect of customs tariff." Both Tupper and Dufferin signed the treaty.

In other respects Canada's position was much the same in 1914 as in 1867. The doctrine of repugnance still applied to Canadian legislation. The amendment of the constitution remained in British hands. The establishment of the Supreme Court of Canada in 1875 had not altered the position of the Judicial Committee of the Privy Council as Canada's final court of appeal, despite the efforts of Edward Blake to have appeals abolished. Canadians had played some part in the negotiation of treaties; but Canada had not secured control of high policy involving the ultimate decisions of peace and war. When Great Britain declared war on Germany in 1914, it was taken for granted in Britain and Canada that the dominion was at war also.

— 5 —

CANADA COMES OF AGE, 1914-1945

World War I. In many ways Canada matured as a result of World War I. The Canadian contribution to the Allied campaigns against Germany was impressive, and the Canadian economy and Canadian national sentiment developed together. War came with the Conservatives in office. The administration under Robert Laird Borden (1854-1937), a Halifax lawyer, had been elected to power in 1911. Borden's government gave vigorous support to the war effort. Before the end of 1914, the first contingent of the Canadian Expeditionary Force had been despatched to England, and, by 1916, four Canadian divisions were serving in the Allied armies in France. Canada's citizen troops in France had a very good record. They served with especial distinction at the second and third battles of Ypres, at Courcelette, Vimy Ridge, Passchendaele, and the second battle of Mons. In June, 1917, Sir Arthur Currie, a Canadian, succeeded Sir Julian Byng in command of the Canadian Corps. Canadians comprised a large part of the Royal Flying Corps and contributed several of the leading flying aces. Billy Bishop shot down seventy-two German planes. Canada had over 500,000 men in arms, sent overseas 425,000 and lost 60,000 war dead.

The war effected a considerable expansion of the Canadian economy. Canadian mineral production was increased from just under 129 million dollars in 1914 to 211.3 million in 1918. Wartime demand for shells and semi-fabricated steel products led to a substantial expansion of Canada's steel industry. There was rapid development of agriculture and other raw material industries.

Wheat acreage in the Prairie Provinces increased by 80
per cent in the period 1913-1919. Exports of meat increased from a total of six million dollars in 1913 to
eighty-five million in 1919. Total Canadian exports rose
from 355 million dollars in 1913 to 1,216 in 1919. The
war was financed mainly by taxation and by internal loans
which, according to the Sirois Report (volume 1, pages
97-100), were made available by an inflationary credit
policy. War finance brought about a rapid development
of Canadian financial institutions; the sale of 2,000 million dollars of war loan bonds gave a tremendous stimulus
to security writing and distribution.

Conscription and the Union Government.   An unfortunate result of the war, especially for the Conservatives, was the widening of the divergence between French
and English in Canada. Laurier had been able to carry
many of his compatriots in support of a moderate war
effort in the 1914-1916 period. By 1917, in view of the
increasing difficulty of voluntary recruiting, the government began to contemplate "conscription," or compulsory
military service. To this the French, including Laurier,
were unalterably opposed. When the Military Service Act
was introduced by Borden in June, 1917 and passed, the
Liberal party split "along the line of the Ottawa River."
A considerable part of the Anglo-Saxon wing of the Liberals entered a coalition with Borden in October, 1917.
The coalition, under the title of the Union Government,
won a bitter general election fought on the conscription
issue, in December, 1917. The election came close to
isolating the French. Of the one hundred and fifty-three
government members only three were from Quebec, while
the Liberals elected sixty-two members in that Province.
There were serious riots in Quebec City in March and
April, 1918 in protest against conscription. There were
also demonstrations by English-speaking workmen in
Winnipeg and by farmers in southwestern Ontario, but
the most serious breach was between French and English.

After the war, the rise of farmer and labour protest
movements in western Canada and in Ontario and the
revival of Liberalism helped to drive the Conservatives
from power. In 1920, Sir Robert Borden was succeeded
as Prime Minister by Hon. Arthur Meighen, under whom

the Union Government became a straight Conservative administration. In the election on December 6, 1921, the Conservatives were decisively defeated, obtaining only forty-nine seats. Of these, thirty-seven were in Ontario. During the prosperous years of the twenties, the country was therefore under the control of the Liberals, led by William Lyon Mackenzie King (1874-1950).

Western Labour Movement. In the decade after 1918, radical movements of protest were a feature of Canadian life. They were the result of industrial and agricultural expansion and were particularly identified with the west. The western labour movement had begun toward the end of the nineteenth century, and by 1912 about a third of the locals in Canada were located in the west. The intellectual leaders of the western labour movement in the period following World War I were a group of freethinkers and Christian liberals, chiefly immigrants from the British Isles, living mainly in Winnipeg. The group included R. B. Russell, R. J. Johns, Fred Dixon, John Queen, William Ivens, R. Durward, and J. S. Woodsworth. Woodsworth and Ivens were former Protestant ministers. Many of the group were Socialists, but their socialism was adapted to the syndicalism of such British leaders as H. M. Hyndman of the Social Democratic Federation, Tom Mann and James Connolly. Fred Dixon, while not a Socialist, agreed with the others in his sympathy for labour. The old countrymen were more freethinking than the Canadians like Woodsworth, who were closer to their Christian origins.

The One Big Union and the Winnipeg General Strike. A number of western labour leaders, including Russell and Johns, participated in 1918-1919 in the attempt to organize the One Big Union. The O.B.U. represented a revolt of western labour against the dominance of eastern trade unionists. It was based upon the principle of establishing a single large union which would include all the workers in Canada—manual and white collar. Before the organization of the O.B.U. had gone far, its leaders and other members of the Winnipeg labour movement became involved in the Winnipeg General Strike. It was a dramatic and bitter struggle which lasted from May 15 to June 25, 1919. The strike was the culmination of a

movement of unrest, the result of postwar reaction, infla-
tion, developing unemployment, and resentment against
profiteering. The utterances of labour radicals within and
outside the O.B.U. had given a new militancy to western
labour. The immediate cause was a dispute in the building
and metal trades which ended in the calling of a general
strike by the Winnipeg Trades and Labour Council. Between twenty-five and thirty thousand workers went out.
The strike was notable for the remarkable discipline on
the part of the strikers during its first three weeks. It
spread, to a limited extent, to Vancouver and other western cities. It eventually collapsed after the arrest of the
leaders on June 17 and the intervention of police and
troops to suppress the "riot" of June 21. The strike leaders were afterwards tried on a charge of seditious conspiracy and given sentences varying from six months to
two years. In the opinion of the writer, the strike was
not a seditious conspiracy, but it was an effort to establish
the principle of collective bargaining. Partly as a result
of the trials, the strike left a legacy of great bitterness in
Winnipeg. The O.B.U. gained in popularity from the
strike in 1919. However, by the end of 1921, opposition
from craft unionism reduced it to a factor of slight importance. Of greater long-run significance was the impetus
which the strike gave to the Independent Labour Party of
Manitoba, which was formed in 1920. It was an important
precursor of the C.C.F., or Co-operative Commonwealth
Federation.

   The Progressive Movement.   While western labour
was active and militant, prairie farmers were organizing
the Progressive Party, a comparatively brief phenomenon
in Canadian political life. The movement was strongly
supported in Ontario, where the farmers resented the
tariff, rural depopulation, and conscription. In large measure the Progressives represented a western revolt against
eastern metropolitan dominance. Western farmers envisaged the Canadian economy as designed by the control
of tariffs, railways, and credit to draw wealth from the
west into Ontario and Quebec. They regarded the old-
line political parties as means to implement this policy
and accordingly attempted to form a new farmer-domi-
nated party. They demanded reductions in tariffs and

freight rates and revision of bank legislation. The Progressive movement was a further step in the organization of Canadian farmers, which had begun formally with the establishment of the Canadian Council of Agriculture in 1909. In the years between 1918 and 1921, the Progressives achieved considerable success at the polls. Provincial parties reflecting Progressive views captured power: the United Farmers of Ontario in 1919, the United Farmers of Alberta in 1921, and the United Farmers of Manitoba in 1922. The National Progressive Party was organized at Winnipeg in January, 1920, with T. A. Crerar as leader. The party elected sixty-five members to the federal parliament in the election of 1921.

The Progressives achieved distinct success in the parliamentary session of 1922-1925. Largely as a result of their influence, the Liberal Government implemented substantial reduction in the tariff in 1924 and re-established the Crow's Nest Pass Agreement, limiting freight rates on certain commodities carried to and from the west. The Progressives failed to secure the reforms which they desired in bank legislation: the introduction of annual charters and a 7 per cent limit on interest. The Progressive Party was fatally divided from the beginning. One wing, chiefly identified with Alberta and with Henry Wise Wood (1860-1941), regarded the party as exclusively a farmers' group and favoured considerable independence on the part of individual M.P.'s. The other wing, chiefly identified with Manitoba and T. A. Crerar, was anxious to secure support from elements other than the farmers and laid greater emphasis upon party discipline. Mainly as a result of this division, the federal Progressives soon began to lose ground and by 1930 had disappeared from federal politics. The provincial farmer governments were defeated in Ontario in 1923, and in Alberta in 1935. The Manitoba farmer administration retained office, but under John Bracken became increasingly identified with liberalism. While unsuccessful in establishing a permanent party, the Progressives exercised a profound influence on Canadian political life. W. L. Morton, in his volume, *The Progressive Party in Canada,* describes their success in securing a more general recognition of western grievances. In the west itself they developed a body of opinion which

was later available for other protest movements, the
C.C.F. and Social Credit.

The Twenties. Canada was for the most part prosperous in the decade of the twenties; it was a time of
expansion and of further diversification of the Canadian
economy. While the Maritime Provinces profited little
from the general prosperity, Ontario and Quebec achieved
great expansion. Water-power development increased
from a capacity of 2 million to 4.8 million horsepower
during the decade, while there was heavy capital investment in electric stations, pulp and paper factories, and
mines. Four-fifths of tourist spending, which reached 300
million dollars in 1929, was in Ontario and Quebec.

A milder boom was experienced in the Prairie Provinces where improved acreage increased by 21 per cent
between 1926 and 1931. In the decade of the 1920's, railway mileage in the Prairie Provinces increased by nearly
2,900 miles. An important development occurred in the
wheat industry with the organization of co-operative selling agencies, the wheat pools. Provincial pools were
organized in the three Prairie Provinces in 1923 and
combined to form a central sales agency, the Canadian
Co-operative Wheat Producers Limited. During the years
1925-1928, the pools secured a membership of over half
the western farmers and paid slightly higher prices for
wheat than those received by non-pool farmers.

British Columbia experienced a rapid development
based on new sources of power (electricity and oil), new
industrial metals, and a growing demand for wood pulp.
Despite this great prosperity, the Canadian economy, so
largely dependent on the export of primary products, was
particularly vulnerable to fluctuations in world trade.

Mackenzie King Liberalism, 1921-1930. The central feature of Canadian political history during this
period was the revival of the Liberal Party. Presiding
over the party was W. L. Mackenzie King, who had been
elected leader in 1919. He was destined to be the dominant personality in Canadian politics for the next thirty
years. Mr. King was a rather inscrutable character. He
combined a capacity for high-sounding rhetoric with
great political shrewdness. The central purpose of Mr.
King's career was to preserve the unity of Canada and of

the Liberal Party. He was determined also to promote the cause of Canadian autonomy within the Empire. Certain of Mr. King's characteristics helped to make him the great unifier in Canada. They also exasperated his opponents. He had a great capacity for procrastination in the face of difficult problems, such as dominion-provincial relations and the flag issue. He often avoided firm positions from which retreat would be difficult. He had a flair for sensing Canadian public opinion. Under his sure touch, the Liberal Party became a comprehensive, all-things-to-all-men aggregation in which people of considerable diversities of opinion could find their political home.

Mr. King's tenure of office began in 1921, when he was able to capitalize on the postwar unpopularity of the Conservatives to return 116 members out of a total of 235. Tariff reductions, restoration of the Crow's Nest Pass Agreement and Progressive dissensions enabled Mr. King to win back farmer support in the West in 1925 and 1926. The distinctive feature of his career in this period was his championship of Canadian autonomy at the Imperial Conferences of 1923 and 1926. In 1926 Mr. King became involved in a notable controversy with the governor-general, Lord Byng. The question at issue was whether the governor-general was within his rights in refusing the Prime Minister's request for a dissolution of parliament. The propriety of Mr. King's action in requesting a dissolution was open to doubt. He resigned on June 28, 1926 and was succeeded by the Conservatives under Hon. Arthur Meighen, but in the election of September 14, 1926, the Liberals were returned to office. Mr. King was finally defeated in the election of July, 1930, but the Conservatives achieved power only to be confronted with the great depression.

The Depression. The prosperity of the twenties ended with the onset of the great depression, which was felt by Canada in common with much of the rest of the world in the period 1929-1939. Canada was particularly vulnerable to fluctuations of prices in world markets since a third of its income came directly from exports. Two-thirds of these exports consisted of raw materials such as foodstuffs, newsprint, lumber, and minerals, the prices of which fluctuated widely. Many features of the Canadian economy—its transportation system, processing plants, and factories for the production of implements and machines—were tied in with the export trade. Much of the capital used to develop the country had been borrowed abroad and involved interest payments which had to be kept up in good times and bad.

The onset of the depression in Canada is strikingly described in volume one of the *Sirois Report*. Agriculture and the various lumber industries were particularly affected by a catastrophic fall in prices. The Canadian income from exports, after meeting interest payments on foreign loans, fell from $1,500 million in 1928-1929 to $580 million in 1932-1933. Rigidities such as fixed interest charges and salaries shielded some Canadians; prices of tariff-protected manufactures did not decline as much as farm prices. The incidence of the depression fell mainly upon primary producers, the unemployed, and investors in stocks. Regions like Saskatchewan and Alberta were especially hard hit. The wheat pools were soon on the verge of bankruptcy. As a result, the Dominion Government in 1935 assumed control of the central selling agency. By the Canada Wheat Board Act of 1935 a board of grain commissioners was established to control sales of wheat, while the pools continued as voluntary agencies.

Progress of the Labour Movement. During the twenties and thirties, progress was made in the organizing of unskilled and semiskilled workers on an industrial rather than a craft basis. A start was made in this direction by the formation of the All-Canadian Congress of Labour in 1927. Industrial unionism was considerably extended in the 1930's by the vigorous organizing activities of unions affiliated with the American Congress of Industrial Organizations, formed in 1935. They were especially active in such industries as steel, automobiles, rubber, electrical manufacturing, and metal-mining. Expelled from the Trades and Labour Congress of Canada, these unions combined with the All-Canadian Congress to form the Canadian Congress of Labour in 1940.

The Bennett Administration. The Conservatives were unfortunate in being confronted with the problems of the depression when they succeeded to office in August,

1930. The new Prime Minister was R. B. Bennett (1870-1947), a Calgary lawyer. He was able, vigorous, and dictatorial, and dominated his cabinet to an unusual extent. Mr. Bennett proposed to cure the depression by a policy of higher protection and sound money and by "blasting" his way into the markets of the world. He undertook to "end unemployment." Unfortunately for the administration, unemployment was not ended, and Canadian exports continued to decline. The federal government did little to improve the position of the exporters. In monetary policy, Mr. Bennett avoided expedients like credit expansion and currency depreciation which western producers of primary products for export were anxious to have implemented. Large additions to the tariff in 1930 shielded the manufacturer by holding up the prices of his products; but this added to the burdens of the exporter. The administration achieved some constructive legislation. It began two important ventures in state control, the Canadian Radio Broadcasting Commission in 1932 [2] and the Bank of Canada in 1934.

Despite his vigour and optimism, the depression was too much for Mr. Bennett. By 1935, he had become extremely unpopular, particularly in the west, which resented his supposed failure to consider the interests of the western farmer. Bennett's "New Deal," an ambitious programme of social legislation, was introduced in the House of Commons in 1935. The programme was concerned with minimum wages, maximum hours of work, and social insurance against unemployment. It came too late to enable Mr. Bennett to recapture lost ground and, indeed, alienated right-wing support in eastern Canada. Bennett's feud with one of his colleagues, the Hon. H. H. Stevens (b. 1878), over the Price Spreads Commission in 1934 led to the formation of the Reconstruction Party and further weakened the Conservatives. They were decisively beaten in the election on October 14, 1935, and the country entered upon a long period of Liberal administration.

The Co-operative Commonwealth Federation. During the depression, two political parties of protest were

---

[2] In 1936 it was replaced by the Canadian Broadcasting Corporation.

founded, the Co-operative Commonwealth Federation and
the Social Credit Party. These parties were joint heirs to
the old Progressive Party. The C.C.F. was an attempt to
form a social democratic party out of farmer and labour
elements. In Saskatchewan farm leaders in 1931 agreed
to work with the Saskatchewan Labour Party, headed by
M. J. Coldwell. The two groups undertook to form a
farmer-labour party with a socialist programme. Labour
elements in other western cities, especially Winnipeg and
Vancouver, provided additional support for this movement. The Independent Labour Party of Manitoba had
been established in 1920, and two of its members, J. S.
Woodsworth and A. A. Heaps, were in the federal parliament. The League for Social Reconstruction, modelled on
the English Fabians, was formed in January, 1932, by
eastern university teachers. These elements combined at
the Calgary Convention of August, 1932, to establish the
C.C.F. with Woodsworth as its first leader. A year later
the party adopted a formal programme, contained in the
Regina Manifesto. (*See Reading No. 20.*) The programme
was a compromise between doctrinaire socialism and the
traditional individualism of the eastern farmer. It provided for socialization of the means of production and
"security of tenure for the farmer upon his farm."

After 1933 the progress of the C.C.F. was appreciable
but not overwhelming. The party achieved its greatest
successes in rural and urban areas in Saskatchewan. It
also became firmly established in the Winnipeg and Vancouver areas where labour was strong. S. M. Lipset in his
volume, *Agrarian Socialism,* has shown that the party
made its earliest gains in Saskatchewan, among fairly
prosperous farmer and labour elements. In federal politics seven members of the C.C.F. were elected to the
House of Commons in 1935, eight in 1940, twenty-eight
in 1945, twenty-three in 1953, and twenty-five in 1957.
The party achieved success in provincial politics in Saskatchewan, Ontario, and British Columbia. It captured
power in Saskatchewan in 1944.

Social Credit. The second heir to the Progressive
movement was the Social Credit Party, which developed
in Alberta in the early thirties. Led by William Aberhart,
a schoolteacher and radio evangelist, the Social Credit

group defeated the United Farmers of Alberta to capture
control of the provincial government in the election of
1935. Social Credit was partly the product of the Prairie
environment. Social Crediters, like other westerners, were
dissatisfied with the debtor-creditor relationship with eastern Canada. They shared the traditional western discon-
tent with freight rates, tariffs, and the old-line parties.
From the United Farmers of Alberta the Social Crediters
inherited the ideas of a one-party political system, cabinet
dominance over the legislature, and direct democracy exercised through annual delegate conventions. The programme of the Social Credit Party was largely derived
from Major William Douglas, a British engineer, who
exercised great influence over Aberhart. C. B. Macpherson, in *Democracy in Alberta,* has described Major Douglas's panaceas. Major Douglas believed that the economic
ills of society were mainly the result of insufficient purchasing power. He proposed to increase purchasing power
by the extension of "social credit," secured by the productive resources of the province. With these economic
ideas Douglas combined political theory suggestive of
Rousseau's General Will. The people were to endorse a
few general slogans like "End poverty in Alberta," leaving
the application of the system to the "experts." Aberhart
took over Douglas's general ideas but told the people
more about "methods" than would have been approved
by Douglas. The Social Credit movement was neo-
conservative in its repudiation of socialism. Its conservatism was largely the result of the religious background of
Aberhart and many of his associates. They reflected the
political conservatism of evangelical Christianity and its
dislike of root and branch reform.

Aberhart's administration gave honest and efficient government but did not apply social credit theory, mainly
because of constitutional limitations to the power of a
provincial government. In the autumn of 1935 Aberhart
broke with Douglas, who regarded Aberhart's monetary
policies as too orthodox. In 1937 there was a threatened
insurrection in the Social Credit Party in protest against
Aberhart's failure to establish Social Credit. The Premier
then set up the Social Credit Board and passed a series
of acts designed to establish Social Credit. The acts were

quickly disallowed by the federal government. The Social
Credit Board was abolished in 1948. The Social Credit
government was able to assume the position of the great
opponent of socialism in the west. This was a rewarding
position for the purposes of vote-getting in Alberta and
of conducting financial operations in eastern Canada.
Aberhart died in 1943 and was succeeded as Premier of
Alberta by E. C. Manning. In the federal field, the successes of the Social Credit Party were confined almost
entirely to Alberta until 1953, when four of its members
were elected in British Columbia as well as eleven in
Alberta. Social Credit Members of Parliament devoted
their speeches to the exposition of Social Credit theories
and to denunciations of big money interests and of com-
munists. They were more doctrinaire in their adherence
to Major Douglas's ideas than were the group in office in
Alberta.

   French Canadian Nationalism.   While new parties
of protest developed in the west, a recurrent protest, that
of French-Canadian nationalism, was revived in Quebec
after 1914. It was fostered by resentment against the
position of the French language in the Ontario schools.
In 1912, the Ontario Department of Education issued a
regulation requiring English as the sole language of instruction, with minor exceptions, in the elementary schools
of the province. The breach between French and English
Canadians during the First World War gave fresh impetus
to French nationalism. Its chief organ was *L'Action Fran-
çaise,* which began publication in 1917. The guiding
spirit of the movement was Canon Lionel Groulx, who
had become Professor of History at the University of
Montreal in 1914. He became editor of *L'Action Fran-
çaise* in 1920. Although the movement tended to decline
in the late twenties, it revived again during the depression.

   The principal beneficiary of French nationalism during the late part of the depression was Maurice Duplessis,
who became leader of the Quebec Conservatives in 1931.
In 1935 he combined forces with Paul Gouin, who had
just formed *L'Action Nationale Liberale,* a youth movement. Eventually Gouin broke with Duplessis, but Duplessis retained most of Gouin's support. The Duplessis party
was now named *L'Union Nationale.* Duplessis cultivated

English-Canadian, British, and American business interests. Despite his hostility toward organized labour he
retained much popular French-Canadian support by making himself the champion of provincial rights in opposition to the federal government. In 1936 *L'Union Nationale* won a majority in the Quebec election and assumed control of the provincial government.

Dominion-Provincial Relations. Quebec insistence
upon provincial rights was merely one aspect of dominion-
provincial relations, which remained a major problem in
Canada in the years after 1920. The Judicial Committee
of the Privy Council continued to bring down decisions
favourable to the provinces as in the Board of Commerce
case (1919-1922). In 1919 the dominion parliament
passed an act to establish a Board of Commerce and
attempted to give the Board power to prevent hoarding
of food, clothing, and fuel. When the matter came before
the Privy Council, the legislation was held to be beyond
the powers of the dominion as it interfered with "property
and civil rights." In explaining the decision, Lord Haldane
indicated that the Judicial Committee still placed narrow
limits on the powers of the dominion government. He
admitted that under certain circumstances wide powers
should be given to the dominion under the "peace, order,
and good government" clause; but the only circumstances
which he mentioned were "war or famine." One important decision, that in regard to the control of radio, was
made in favour of the dominion in 1932.

Political developments in the years between 1921 and
1930 also strengthened the position of the provinces. They
were encouraged by the dominion government to undertake new responsibilities and other projects of development in highway construction and public utilities. They
also expanded their support of mothers' allowances, old
age pensions, and hospitals. The dominion government
shared the cost of old age pensions. Aggressiveness on
the part of the provinces in pushing their claims was met
by a number of concessions by the dominion. Increased
subsidies were given to the Maritime Provinces as a result
of the recommendations of the Duncan Report in 1927.
In 1928 the Prairie Provinces were given control of their
crown lands. After the report of the Turgeon Commis-

sion, they were awarded compensation for part of their crown lands which had already been alienated. The provinces were consulted in 1930 prior to the passage of the Statute of Westminster in 1931.

The strong constitutional position of the provinces posed a serious financial problem. The federal government had unlimited taxing powers under the B.N.A. Act, while a large part of the spending functions were in the hands of the provinces. The question of how the provinces were to secure adequate financial support within the framework of the constitution became particularly acute during the depression, when they were saddled with much of the burden of unemployment relief. Even in times of prosperity it was difficult to maintain a reasonable equality of public services in all the provinces. Various attempts were made to solve the question of divided powers. The Sirois Commission was appointed by the dominion government in 1937 to consider the problem of dominion-provincial relations. The Commission recommended that the dominion government should give extensive financial assistance to the provinces in return for the surrender of provincial income, corporation taxes, and succession duties. The dominion-provincial conference called to discuss the plan in January, 1941, speedily broke down. During World War II the dominion and provincial governments negotiated agreements which applied the general principle recommended in the Sirois Report. After 1945 the federal government had fair success in negotiating taxation agreements with the provinces. The sole exception was Quebec which, under Mr. Duplessis, remained firmly aloof.

Religious Thought. While Canada faced its political problems, there were significant developments in Canadian religious thought. The trend toward Christian liberalism was speeded up after World War I. It was characterized by a critical attitude toward the Bible, by an optimistic view of the nature of man and by emphasis upon social justice. Typical of the movement toward liberalism was the *Canadian Journal of Religious Thought*, an ably written periodical published in Toronto in the years between 1924 and 1932. Among its contributors were Richard Roberts, G. B. King, A. R. Gordon, and

H. A. Kent. M. G Ross, in his volume *The Y.M.C.A. in Canada*, has indicated how Christian liberalism influenced the Y.M.C.A. in this period. In its origins an evangelical, and to a great extent a missionary, organization, the Y.M.C.A. gradually departed from its original position. Y.M.C.A. leaders were much influenced not only by Christian liberalism but by John Dewey and the implications of his philosophy. In reaction against the liberalism of the larger denominations, the evangelical sects such as the Pentecostals and various Baptist groups increased in strength and numbers, particularly in western Canada. This has been noted in recent works by H. H. Walsh (*The Christian Church in Canada, 1956*) and William E. Mann (*Sect, Cult, and Church in Alberta, 1955*). During the years after 1940, an effort was made in Canada, as elsewhere, to stress some of the doctrines of orthodox Christianity, including the sinfulness of man, which the liberals had tended to ignore. Advocates of this new or neo-orthodox position did not return to the idea of Biblical inspiration, at least in its traditional sense.

    Letters and Art. The period after 1920 was a productive one in Canadian literary culture, particularly in poetry. Like the theologians, many Canadian poets reacted against the standards of the immediate past, both of style and of content. This was particularly true of the Montreal group which included Abraham Klein, Frank Scott, A. J. M. Smith, and Leo Kennedy. The members of this group published the *McGill Fortnightly*. They were all experimenters, eager to naturalize in Canada the kind of poetry written by T. S. Eliot and Ezra Pound. All were zealots for the metaphysical verse of the seventeenth century, which was being reinterpreted in Eliot's criticism. Other Canadian poets of the period were Ralph Gustafson, Robert Finch, Anne Marriot, and Earle Birney. E. J. Pratt, a Newfoundlander and Professor of English at Victoria College, Toronto, wrote vigorous and imaginative narrative poetry, much of it about the sea. Canadian poetry was encouraged by such periodicals as the *Canadian Forum,* the *Northern Review,* and the *Tamarack Review.* An important step in the development of mature criticism in Canada was the annual publication beginning in 1935 of an extended critique, "Letters in Canada," by

the *University of Toronto Quarterly*. Equally significant
was the publication in 1943 of E. K. Brown's critical
study, *On Canadian Poetry*.

A unique style in the painting of the Canadian landscape was developed by Tom Thomson (1877-1917),
whose most famous picture was entitled *Jack Pine*.
Thomson's pictures identified Canada with the scenery of
the Great Canadian Shield. He provided the inspiration
for the school of painters known as the Group of Seven.

Development of Canadian Autonomy. One of the
most important features of Canadian political history
since 1914 was the virtual completion of Canada's progress toward practical independence. As a result of the
size and effectiveness of its contribution in World War I,
Canada secured important recognition as an autonomous
country. This was partly a result of vigorous protests
from Sir Robert Borden in 1916. He had become dissatisfied with the failure of the British government to
keep Canada informed respecting the conduct of the war.
Canada and the other dominions were included in the
Imperial War Cabinet which was established in 1917. In
describing its functions, Mr. Lloyd George, the Prime
Minister of the United Kingdom, declared that "the responsible heads of the government of the Empire—should
meet together at regular intervals to confer about foreign
policy and matters connected therewith." Canada was
represented at the Versailles Peace Conference in 1919
and signed the peace treaties as a separate power.

In the years between 1919 and 1939, the effort to
achieve complete autonomy became a crusade with many
Canadians. The influence of university teachers such as
F. H. Underhill at Toronto, and A. R. M. Lower at
United College, Winnipeg, was exerted in support of
the movement. J. W. Dafoe and G. V. Ferguson, both
of the *Winnipeg Free Press,* were powerful advocates of
Canadian autonomy. O. D. Skelton, the Under-Secretary
of State for External Affairs, trained a generation of
"bright young men" who reflected his nationalism. Conservative and Liberal politicians both played their parts
in the movement toward autonomy. In 1921 Arthur
Meighen, the Conservative Prime Minister, went beyond
the principle of Canadian autonomy to the point where

he exerted an important influence over British foreign policy. At the Imperial Conference of 1921, Meighen took a very independent line against the Anglo-Japanese Treaty and almost single-handed persuaded the British Government not to renew the agreement. Mackenzie King's championship of Canadian autonomy has already been noted. In the Chanak crisis of 1922, he made it clear that Canada would not automatically underwrite British commitments in Europe and elsewhere. Canada's long attempt to secure the treaty-making power culminated in 1923, when Mr. King's colleague, Ernest Lapointe, signed the halibut treaty with the United States as the sole plenipotentiary representing the king. Resolutions adopted at the Imperial Conferences of 1923 and 1926, particularly the Balfour Declaration of 1926, went far toward recognizing the autonomy of the dominions. The Statute of Westminster of 1931 established the principle that legislation of Canada and the other dominions was no longer null and void if it conflicted with legislation passed by the parliament of the United Kingdom. (*See Reading No. 21.*)

Canada's entry into World War II in 1939 marked a further development in Canadian autonomy. In 1914 Great Britain's declaration of war had been assumed to involve Canada automatically. In 1939 Canada was officially neutral until the Canadian declaration on September 10, a week after the British entry. The agreement negotiated with the United States at Ogdensburg in 1940 indicated that Canada had assumed the function of negotiating defence agreements with countries outside the Empire. The strength of Canadian opinion in favour of autonomy was indicated by the reaction to a speech by the British Ambassador to the United States, Lord Halifax, at Toronto in January, 1944. Lord Halifax advocated greater centralization of the Empire and provoked a storm of protest in Canada. The ideas of Lord Halifax were repudiated by Mr. King in a notable address to a joint session of the British parliament on May 11, 1944. (*See Reading No. 22.*) Appeals from Canadian courts to the Judicial Committee of the Privy Council were abolished in criminal cases in 1935. Delivering the judgment of the Judicial Committee of the Privy Council in *British*

Coal Corporation v. *The King*, Lord Sankey stated that
he saw no reason why the federal parliament could not,
in view of the Statute of Westminster, abolish appeals in
criminal cases. Appeals in civil cases were abolished in
1949. In 1949, by an amendment to the British North
America Act, the dominion parliament was empowered
to amend the constitution in matters affecting the dominion government only. After 1949, the only important
limitation on Canada's complete self-government was the
function of the British parliament to amend the British
North America Act in matters affecting both the dominion
and the provinces.

      Canadian Foreign Policy, 1918-1939. In foreign
policy Canada was mainly occupied with the establishment of her status as an autonomous country; otherwise,
the dominion did not take a strong line. Many Canadians
regarded the League of Nations as an effective guarantee
of world peace; but Canadian policy tended to weaken
the League by coolness to the inclusion of effective sanctions in the Covenant. To some extent, Canada served
as a spokesman in the League for American isolationism.
In the critical ten years before 1939, Canada followed the
example of the League countries in failing to advocate
strong measures to check aggression. During the Sino-
Japanese crisis of 1931-1932, Canadian policy was in-
decisive. When Mussolini attacked Ethiopia in 1935,
Canadian diplomacy was extremely cautious. W. A. Riddell, the Canadian delegate to the League, sponsored a
motion providing for the imposition of sanctions on the
sale of oil and other war material to Italy; but his action
was repudiated by Ernest Lapointe, the acting Prime
Minister. Like many other western countries, Canada did
little to rearm until shortly before the outbreak of war
in 1939. The regular army in 1939 numbered only about
forty-five hundred soldiers.

      The negative character of Canadian policy during this
period was in large measure a result of grave differences
in Canadian public opinion over the issue of Canadian
participation in another European war. Four distinct
schools of thought were apparent. Complete pacifists
favoured peace at any price. Isolationists insisted that
it would be in Canada's interests to maintain a policy

of neutrality. Supporters of the League of Nations favoured Canadian participation in a war in defence of the collective system. Exponents of the "ready-aye-ready" viewpoint believed that Canada should participate in any war in which Britain was involved. With the outbreak of war in September, 1939, each of the groups reacted characteristically, but in parliament support of Canada's declaration of war was almost unanimous. When parliament was convened on September 10, opposition to Canada's entry came only from the C.C.F. leader, J. S. Woodsworth. Woodsworth broke with other members of his party on the issue.

World War II: the Armed Services. The Second World War exercised a maturing effect on Canada similar to that of World War I. The Canadian war programme was greater in scope than that of the first war. The total enlistment of the Canadian army was 730,000 of which 630,000 served in the active army. (C. P. Stacey, *The Canadian Army 1939-1945*, Ottawa, 1948.) Its record was excellent although, through no fault of the Canadians, two of the actions in which it was involved were disastrous: the fall of Hong Kong in December, 1941, and the Dieppe raid of August, 1942. The First Canadian Corps fought for twenty months in the Italian campaign, which began with the landing in Sicily in July, 1943. The Third Canadian Division participated in the Normandy landing on June 6, 1944. The Second Corps, under General Guy Simonds, engaged in the desperate fighting which culminated in the closing of the Falaise Gap in August, 1944. In the autumn of 1944 the Canadian Army, under General H. D. G. Crear, cleared the Channel ports, and later opened the Scheldt estuary. The Canadian Army included some British troops. In March, 1945, it was joined by the First Canadian Corps, which had been transferred from Italy. In the spring of 1945 the Canadians participated in the clearing of the Rhineland, the liberation of the Netherlands, and the destruction of Hitler's empire.

The record of the other services was equally distinguished. The Royal Canadian Air Force was expanded from a personnel of 4,000 in 1939 to over 206,000 by the end of 1943. It played a major role in the war against

Germany. In addition, Canada developed and administered the British Commonwealth Air Training Plan. The Plan provided 131,553 trained airmen for the Royal Air Force and the air forces of the dominions. The Canadian navy rendered vital service to the Allied cause, chiefly in escorting vessels on the North Atlantic run. By the end of 1944 nearly 5,000 Canadians were attached to the Newfoundland command, which was in charge of this convoy duty.

World War II: Economic and Political Record. Canadian industrial expansion was on a par with the increase in the armed services. Aircraft production and shipbuilding experienced large increases in output; while several new branches of manufacturing, such as those of roller bearings, magnesium, and high octane gas, were established for the first time in Canada. Canadian steel output increased between 1939 and 1942-1944 by about 120 per cent and aluminum output by about 500 per cent.

As in World War I, the recruiting issue caused political difficulties in regard to French Canada, which displayed its traditional hostility to conscription for overseas service. The Liberal government began conscription for home service in the summer of 1940. On April 27, 1942, the famous conscription plebiscite was held. The voters were asked to indicate whether they would release the government from its pledge not to resort to conscription for overseas service. The government was given the required mandate, although Quebec voted "no." However, none of the conscripts were sent overseas until the last year of the war. In November, 1944, a shortage of infantry recruits and resultant demands from Col. J. L. Ralston (1881-1948), the Minister of Defence, produced a sharp political crisis. The crisis culminated in the decision of the government to send 16,000 conscripts to Europe. This decision produced riots in Montreal, but the ending of hostilities prevented the crisis from becoming more serious.

— 6 —

CONCLUSION: CANADA SINCE 1945

Political Developments after World War II. For twelve years after World War II Canadian politics was dominated by the Liberals, who were returned to power in the elections of 1945, 1949, and 1953. The Liberals continued to occupy the position of a moderate, middle-of-the-road party. The *bonne entente* between French and English was its basic principle. The Liberals identified themselves with an external policy essentially in Canada's interests and professedly not prejudiced by emotional loyalties to objects outside Canada. They balanced moderate protection for industry with price supports for agricultural commodities, particularly wheat. In the sphere of dominion-provincial relations, they continued to press for taxation agreements which would redress the disparity between "have" and "have-not" provinces. Unlike the Liberal Party of the nineteenth century, the modern Canadian Liberals did not stress freedom or constitutionalism. They showed slight concern for the privileges of parliament in the debates on the Emergency Powers Bill in 1955 and the Pipe Line Bill in 1956. More radical than liberal, they sponsored measures of social amelioration. The principal landmarks in this programme were the Unemployment Insurance Act of 1940, the Family Allowances Act of 1944, and the Old Age Security Act of 1951. An amendment to the B.N.A. Act in 1940 added unemployment insurance to the powers of the federal parliament. The succession of Louis St. Laurent as Liberal leader and Prime Minister in 1948 did not involve any major alterations of policy. St. Laurent was more forth-right and less adroit than Mackenzie King, but, prior to the election of 1957, he was equally successful at the polls.

In the years after 1945 many Conservatives continued to retain their traditional loyalties and antipathies. Conservative loyalism received considerable stimulus from royal tours in 1939 and 1951, World War II, and the Battle of Britain. Conservatism still showed itself in its insistence upon the preservation of the title "Dominion" of Canada, and upon retaining the Union Jack as at least part of the national flag. The Conservatives failed to make much progress with the French. The party had never recovered from the loss of the French bloc between 1885 and 1896. The breach had been widened by the conscription crises of 1917 and 1944-1945. For over twenty years after 1935 the Conservatives were unsuccessful in federal politics. John Bracken was leader from 1942 to 1948, and George Drew led the party from 1948 to 1956, but neither was able to displace the Liberals. Under John Diefenbaker the party secured 111 seats, out of a total of 265, in the election of 1957. The Conservatives took office as a minority government. The number of Liberals in the House of Commons was reduced from 172 to 107. The failure of the Liberals was the result of a number of factors. Many Canadians resented the use of closure by the Liberals in the debate on the Pipe Line Bill in 1956. The Liberals were regarded as too complacent in their attitude toward foreign economic penetration of Canada. They were thought to be insufficiently concerned with the interests of the common man. They were charged with failure to reduce taxes and interest rates and with failure to increase old age pensions. Western farmers were dissatisfied with the government's wheat policy. The Liberals were regarded by many of the voters as overconfident and domineering. (*See Reading No. 24.*)

Other Political Parties. The C.C.F. showed a high level of ability in its parliamentary group which included M. J. Coldwell, Stanley Knowles, Angus McInnis, and Clarie Gillis. The party, however, failed to achieve any considerable electoral success except in Saskatchewan. There were indications that the party was modifying its

doctrinaire socialism. The revised manifesto of 1956 was
very critical of capitalism; but it was less sweeping than
the Regina Manifesto of 1933 in its proposals to socialize
the means of production. The party retained its concern
for social justice. Members of the Social Credit Party in
the federal parliament continued to expound their traditional monetary arguments. Since they were in opposition, they could afford to be more doctrinaire in this
regard than the Social Crediters in power in Alberta and
British Columbia, where the party had been elected to
office in 1952.

In Quebec, Mr. Duplessis and the *Union Nationale*
were in opposition during World War II. Mr. Duplessis
was returned to office in 1944 and continued to dominate
Quebec provincial politics in the period following the war.
He functioned in a society which was being subjected to
great strains and stresses by the process of industrializa-
tion. Among its repercussions was a new militancy on
the part of French-Canadian trade-unions. This was indicated by the Asbestos Strike of 1949. There was evidence of a growing social conscience and of a renewed
emphasis upon political morality in French Canada.
Notable exponents of this attitude were the Faculty of
Social Sciences at Laval University and a group called
Le Rassemblement which appeared in 1956. This new
trend was slow to make serious inroads into the voting
strength of the older parties in Quebec politics.

Canada in World Affairs. After 1945 Canada
played an effective role as a middle power, strong enough
to be listened to with respect in the United Nations and
the North Atlantic Treaty Organization. Canada's entry
into the United Nations in 1945 was not attended by
the isolationist sentiments which had weakened its role
in the League of Nations. However, in the atmosphere
of controversy between Russia and the West in the 1945-
1949 period, Canadians gradually lost faith in the United
Nations as a guarantor of world peace. The Canadian
government was active in the negotiations which led to
the formation of the North Atlantic Treaty Organization,
or NATO, in 1949 as a more effective defence against
aggression. Canada participated in the Korean War of
1950-1953, maintaining a brigade in the Commonwealth

Division. Canada also played a part of considerable importance in the commissions which were set up in 1954 to supervise the truce in Indochina. After the outbreak of hostilities in the Middle East in October, 1956, the Canadian Secretary of State for External Affairs, L. B. Pearson, was largely responsible for the despatch of the United Nations Expeditionary Force to Egypt. The U.N.E.F. was one important factor in the re-establishment of peace. Mr. Pearson was subsequently awarded the Nobel Peace Prize for 1957. (*See Reading No. 23.*)

Canada's foreign policy is now sufficiently distinct to make possible an analysis of the forces which shape it. An important conditioning factor is the country's geography: its position, terrain, climate, and the character of its natural defences. The size of its economic potential gives Canada weight in the counsels of the world but sets limits to the commitments which it can undertake. Canadian foreign policy is strongly influenced by the nature of the Canadian people. They possess a high degree of technological skill. They have a Christian and liberal-democratic background. They are divided by racial and religious differences, and, like others, they are certain to react against excessive taxation. Canadian foreign policy is conditioned also by relations with outside countries, particularly the United States and Great Britain. Canada has two roles in foreign policy. First, it is an executor of policies previously worked out by the great powers. The Korean War and the Indo-Chinese settlement of 1954 are cases in point. Canada's other role consists in the attempt to find a middle way between powers with divergent views. The Canadian genius for compromise has shown itself in the part played by Canada in the United Nations. A notable example of this ability at compromise was the part played by Canada in the admission of sixteen new member countries to the United Nations in 1955.

The Canadian Achievement. Among the nations of the world, Canada is still a comparatively young country. It is about 350 years since Champlain founded Quebec and 200 since the British conquest. The most obvious achievement has been the settlement of the country from coast to coast and the development of its natural resources: furs, timber, wheat, wood pulp, and minerals. Canada has established an important industrial plant. Much of it, such as meat-packing and paper-manufacturing, is complementary to the primary industries. Canadians also have created a system of transportation and finance to facilitate the process of economic expansion and consolidation. Much of Canada's industrial development is comparatively recent and dates from World Wars I and II. Largely it has been made possible by the tremendous expansion of hydroelectric facilities. Vast iron-ore developments since 1939 have been mainly the result of discoveries in Ontario and in the Quebec Labrador region. By 1952 iron-ore production had reached a figure in excess of five million tons. Canada is an important producer of other minerals: nickel, gold, silver, and asbestos. Pulp and paper has become the country's leading export; it comprised 24 per cent of total Canadian exports in 1954. Canada is the world's second largest producer of aluminum.

Progress of the Canadian labour movement has kept pace with the development of the Canadian economy. At the beginning of 1955 there were over 1,200,000 union members in Canada. Most of the unions were affiliated with a central labour congress. Of these, the three largest were the Trades and Labour Congress of Canada, the Canadian Congress of Labour, and the Canadian and Catholic Confederation of Labour. In April and May, 1956, the Canadian Labour Congress was formed by a merger of the T.L.C. and the C.C.L.

Since Canada is one of the world's major industrial and commercial powers, its population, some fifteen million, appears surprisingly small. It is composed of people of British descent, French Canadians, and Europeans in the approximate proportions of five, three, and two. The last group consists chiefly of Scandinavians, Germans, Italians, Netherlanders, Poles, and Ukrainians. To a large extent they are the immigrants who have come to the country since 1900. The Jewish population, a minority of 200,000, have made a contribution to Canada's development out of all proportion to their numbers.

The political achievements of the Canadians are impressive. Canada has worked out a system of diversity in unity. The Canadian system of federalism has made possible reasonably amicable relations between French and English. Conflicts of interest between the different regions of Canada have been in large measure resolved within the framework of the federation. The French and the English have not always agreed on the issue of civil and religious liberty; but loyal acceptance of judicial decisions has always enabled them to settle their differences. Decisions of the Supreme Court in regard to the Padlock Law and also in regard to the Jehovah's Witnesses are cases in point.

Canadians are proud of their various racial and religious traditions; but they have come to regard themselves primarily as Canadians. They are determined to exist as an independent people and develop their own culture. The Canadian culture is in large measure derivative, but its elements are mingled in unique proportions and are modified by the geography and history of Canada itself. French and English Canadians speak their respective languages; but each is unique in accent and much of its terminology. They share a common affection for the geographic region, Canada, and for the Canadian state with its capital at Ottawa. (*See Reading No. 25.*)

Part II
READINGS

— Reading No. 1 —

CHAMPLAIN'S FIRST ENCOUNTER WITH THE IROQUOIS, 1609[1]

Samuel de Champlain (1567-1635) founded Quebec in 1608 and devoted most of the rest of his life to development of the settlement. He accomplished important explorations in what are now the Maritime Provinces, northern New England, eastern Ontario, and northern New York. In the following excerpt from his Voyages, *Champlain describes his first encounter with the Iroquois in 1609. He had accompanied an Algonquin expedition into the Lake Champlain region.*

✓   ✓   ✓

When evening came we embarked in our canoes to continue on our way; and, as we were going along very quietly, and without making any noise, on the twenty-ninth of the month, we met the Iroquois at ten o'clock at night at the end of a cape that projects into the lake on the west side, and they were coming to war. We both began to make loud cries, each getting his arms ready. We withdrew toward the water, and the Iroquois went ashore and arranged their canoes in line, and began to cut down trees with poor axes, which they get in war sometimes, and also with others of stone; and they barricaded themselves very well.

Our men also passed the whole night with their canoes drawn up close together, fastened to poles, so that they might not get scattered, and might fight all together, if

[1] A. N. Bourne and E. G. Bourne, *The Voyages and Explorations of Samuel de Champlain 1604-1616 Narrated by Himself* (New York, 1906), I, 209-213.

there were need of it; we were on the water within arrow range of the side where their barricades were.

When they were armed and in array, they sent two canoes set apart from the others to learn from their enemies if they wanted to fight. They replied that they desired nothing else; but that, at the moment, there was not much light and that they must wait for the daylight to recognize each other, and that as soon as the sun rose they would open the battle. This was accepted by our men; and while we waited, the whole night was passed in dances and songs, as much on one side as on the other, with endless insults, and other talk, such as the little courage they had, their feebleness and inability to make resistance against their arms, and that when day came they should feel it to their ruin. Our men also were not lacking in retort, telling them that they should see such power of arms as never before; and much other talk, as is customary in the siege of a city. After plenty of singing, dancing, and parleying with one another, daylight came. My companions and I remained concealed for fear that the enemy should see us, preparing our arms the best that we could, separated, however, each in one of the canoes of the Montagnais savages. After arming ourselves with light armor, each of us took an arquebuse and went ashore. I saw the enemy come out of their barricade, nearly 200 men, strong and robust to look at, coming slowly toward us with a dignity and assurance that pleased me very much. At their head there were three chiefs. Our men also went forth in the same order, and they told me that those who wore three large plumes were the chiefs; and that there were only three of them; and that they were recognizable by these plumes, which were a great deal larger than those of their companions; and that I should do all I could to kill them. I promised them to do all in my power, and said that I was very sorry that they could not understand me well, so that I might give order and system to their attack of the enemy, in which case we should undoubtedly destroy them all; but that this could not be remedied; that I was very glad to encourage them and to show them the good-will that I felt, when we should engage in battle.

As soon as we were ashore, they began to run about

200 paces toward their enemy, who were standing firmly and had not yet noticed my companions, who went into the woods with some savages. Our men began to call me with loud cries; and, to give me a passageway, they divided into two parts and put me at their head, where I marched about twenty paces in front of them until I was thirty paces from the enemy. They at once saw me and halted, looking at me, and I at them. When I saw them making a move to shoot at us, I rested my arquebuse against my cheek and aimed directly at one of the three chiefs. With the same shot two of them fell to the ground, and one of their companions, who was wounded and afterwards died. I put four balls into my arquebuse. When our men saw this shot so favorable for them, they began to make cries so loud that one could not have heard it thunder. Meanwhile the arrows did not fail to fly from both sides. The Iroquois were much astonished that two men had been so quickly killed, although they were provided with armor woven from cotton thread and from wood, proof against their arrows. This alarmed them greatly. As I was loading again, one of my companions fired a shot from the woods, which astonished them again to such a degree that, seeing their chiefs dead, they lost courage, took to flight and abandoned the field and their fort, fleeing into the depths of the woods. Pursuing them thither I killed some more of them. Our savages also killed several of them and took ten or twelve of them prisoners. The rest escaped with the wounded. There were fifteen or sixteen of our men wounded by arrow shots, who were soon healed.

After we had gained the victory, they amused themselves by taking a great quantity of Indian corn and meal from their enemies, and also their arms, which they had left in order to run better. And having made good cheer, danced and sung, we returned three hours afterward with the prisoners.

This place, where this charge was made, is in latitude 43 degrees and some minutes, and I named the lake Lake Champlain.

— Reading No. 2 —

NEW FRANCE, 1683-1684[2]

Baron de Lahontan (1616-1716), French soldier and author, came to Canada in 1683 as an officer in the marines. During the winter of 1683-1684, he was quartered at Beaupré, seventeen miles below Quebec. He wrote the following letter to an old relative who gave him annual financial assistance. He was wrong in his chronology in his reference to the Carignan-Salières regiment. It came to Canada in 1665, and several of its companies were disbanded in Canada in 1668.

✓　　　　✓　　　　✓

Letter II Dated at the Canton of Beaupré, May 2, 1684

Sir, As soon as we landed last year, Mr. *de la Barre* lodg'd our three Companies in some Cantons or Quarters in the Neighbourhood of *Quebec*. The Planters call these places *Cotes,* which in *France* signifies no more than the Sea-Coast; tho' in this Country where the names of *Town* and *Village* are unknown, that word is made use of to express a Seignory or Manour, the Houses of which lie at the distance of two or three hundred Paces one from another, and are seated on the brink of the River of St. *Lawrence.* In earnest, Sir, the Boors of those Manors live with more ease and conveniency, than an infinity of the Gentlemen in *France.* I am out indeed in calling 'em

[2] *New Voyages to North America by the Baron de Lahontan. Reprinted from the English edition of 1703 etc. . . .* By Reuben Gold Thwaites, LL.D, 2 vols. I (Chicago, 1905), 34-36, 38.

Boors, for that name is as little known here as in *Spain;*
whether it be that they pay no Taxes, and injoy the liberty
of Hunting and Fishing; or that the easiness of their Life,
puts 'em upon a level with the Nobility. The poorest of
them have four *Arpents* of Ground in front, and thirty or
forty in depth: The whole County being a continued
Forrest of lofty Trees, the stumps of which must be
grub'd up, before they can make use of a Plough. Tis
true, this is a troublesom and chargeable task at first; but
in a short time after they make up their Losses; for when
the Virgin ground is capable of receiving Seed, it yields
an increase to the rate of an hundred fold. Corn is there
sown in *May,* and reap'd about the middle of *September.*
Instead of threshing the Sheafs in the Field, they convey
'em to Barns, where they lie till the coldest season of the
Winter, at which time the Grain is more easily disengag'd
from the Ear. In this Country they likewise sow Pease,
which are much esteem'd in *France.* All sorts of Grain
are very cheap here, as well as Butchers Meat and Fowl.
The price of Wood is almost nothing, in comparison
with the charge of its carriage, which after all is very in-
considerable.

Most of the Inhabitants are a free sort of People that
remov'd hither from *France,* and brought with 'em but
little Money to set up withal: The rest are those who were
Soldiers about thirty or forty years ago, at which time the
Regiment of *Carignan* was broke, and they exchang'd a
Military Post, for the Trade of *Agriculture.* Neither the
one nor the other pay'd any thing for the grounds they
possess, no more than the Officers of these Troops, who
mark'd out to themselves, certain portions of unmanur'd
and woody Lands; for this vast Continent is nothing else
than one continued Forrest. The Governours General
allow'd the Officers three or four Leagues of ground in
front, with as much depth as they pleas'd; and at the
same time the Officers gave the Soldiers as much ground
as they pleas'd, upon the condition of the payment of a
Crown *per Arpent,* by way of Fief. . . .

In this Country everyone lives in a good and a well
furnish'd House; and most of the Houses are of Wood,
and two Stories high. Their Chimneys are very large, by
reason of the prodigious Fires they make to guard them-

selves from the Cold, which is there beyond all measure,
from the Month of *December,* to that of *April.* During
that space of time, the River is always frozen over, notwithstanding the flowing and ebbing of the Sea; and the
Snow upon the ground, is three or four foot deep; which
is very strange in a Country that lies in the Latitude of
forty seven Degrees and some odd Minutes. Most people
impute the extraordinary Snow to the number of Mountains, with which this vast Continent is replenish'd.
Whatever is in that matter, I must take notice of one
thing, that seems very strange, namely that the Summer
days are longer here than at *Paris.*

— Reading No. 3 —

DEBATES ON THE QUEBEC ACT, 1774[3]

Various reasons have been suggested for the passage of the Quebec Act. The debates in the British parliament indicate that the official reason was regard for the rights of the French Canadians.

✓   ✓   ✓

May 26, 1774. LORD NORTH—I wish to give the Right Honorable Member all the satisfaction in my power upon this measure. Respecting the government given to the province, the Honorable Gentleman objects, I suppose, to an Assembly not being appointed. The reason why a Council alone, appointed by the Governor, was preferred, was the small number of English settlers who must chuse that Assembly, in order for their Acts to govern and bind all the French and Roman Catholick subjects. This, Sir, was thought to be very unequal, and even cruel, to have an Assembly, chosen by so small a body, govern so large a one; and if the business is considered maturely, it will, I believe, be found much the most conducive to the happiness of the people. . . . June 10, 1774. Mr. Mackworth moved, "That a clause should be added, allowing of a trial by jury, at the option of either or both of the parties." He recommended the clause as a security for the English in Quebec against the French laws. LORD NORTH opposed it. He recapitulated part of the evidence that had been produced at the Bar, and said Governor

[3] *The History, Debates, and Proceedings of British Houses of Parliament of Great Britain, from the Year 1743 to the Year 1774*, VII (London, 1792), 289, 321-322.

Carleton had informed the House, that the Canadians had
a dislike to the English laws in general; that it was his
opinion, that giving the Canadians their old system of laws
would be the only means of making them a happy people;
that Mr. Hey, the Chief Justice, had said it was his
opinion, that the Canadians, at first, might have been
brought to like the English laws, but since they had been
so indulged, they expected now nothing less than a repeal
of the whole of the laws by which they are governed at
present; and that the Noblesse of the country thought
trial by jury was humiliating and degrading to them, as it
subjected their property to the decision of barbers and
taylors; that Mr. Maseres had, to be sure, said, that juries,
he believed, would be liked under proper regulations, but
the people of Canada did not choose to give their time
and attendance for nothing; that Mons. Lotbiniere, on
a question being put to him, Whether he did not think the
English laws the best for the Canadians in general? said,
"I make no doubt but your laws are good and wise, and
make you a happy people, but I do not think they are
suited to every climate." His Lordship afterwards entered
much upon the subject of juries, and said, the Canadians
could have but a bad opinion of English juries, when a
grand jury there had presented the Roman Catholicks
as a nuisance; he said, the Canadians, in their petition
to the Throne, had desired to have the whole of their
ancient laws restored to them, which this Bill was meant
to do; that in his opinion, the trial by jury was not necessary there; and that, by what he had been informed, the
French laws were sufficient to protect property without it;
that people had very industriously circulated a report
that he had made a Ministerial question of this; he would
assure the House, upon his honor, he had not; that,
after once fixing the government of Quebec, in the hands
of this nation, it was a matter of indifference to him what
law or religion was established, so it made the people
happy; that the British merchants saying their property
would not be secure without English laws, let gentlemen
recollect that British merchants trade to all parts of the
world, and think their property secure in Portugal or
Spain, where they know the Roman Catholick religion is
the religion of the land, and that the number of old or

English subjects in Canada were so few in number, that the cries of 150,000 ought to be given way to in preference of 360.

— Reading No. 4 —

A LOYALIST LETTER, 1776[4]

The bitterness of the Loyalists toward the American Revolutionaries was illustrated in a letter written by Jonathan Sewell from London to his friend, Edward Winslow (1746-1815), on January 10, 1776. During the American Revolution, Winslow was muster-master-general of the British forces in North America. Sewell, a graduate of Harvard and former attorney-general of Massachusetts, had his estate confiscated by the Americans. He went to England in 1775 and in 1787 came out to New Brunswick where he died in 1796. He held the appointment of judge of the admiralty for Nova Scotia until his death.

✓   ✓   ✓

I am out of all patience at hearing, from you and others, the accounts of your Sufferings—what Excuse can be Form'd for a British Admiral, who, with 30 or 40 Ships under his Command, suffers a Garrison to starve tho' surrounded with plenty of every Necessary within the reach of his Ships; who tamely & supinely looks on and sees Fishing Schooners, Whale-boats and Canoes riding triumphant under the Muzzles of his Guns, & carrying off every Supply destined for your relief. Heaven grant you patience, & reward every one according to the Deeds done in the Body. I can tell you for your comfort, that he is cursed as hard on this side of the Water, as he can be on yours—he has now no Advocate here & I believe will scarcely find a Friend in England upon his return. I hope by this time, you are relieved in some measure, as

[4] Rev. W. O. Raymond (ed.), *Winslow Papers A.D. 1776-1826* (New Brunswick Historical Society, Saint John, N. B., 1901), pp. 13-14.

out of the great Number of Ships w'ch have sailed loaded with provisions & Coal, it will be hard indeed, if some don't get in safe, in spite of the Vigilance of the Rebels, & the Inactivity of Trunnion. I verily believe your Sufferings are drawing near a period—you will undoubtedly have, early in the Spring, an Army of 40,000 & a Fleet of upwards of 70 Ships, & then the Mettle of the Rebels will be try'd—hitherto their successes have been owing to their having none to oppose them—the poor infatuated Wretches, as yet, know Nothing of War—they have been treated as froward Children heretofore, but now, they will be treated as incorrigible Traitors. I pity, I feel for the Majority, but, for their Sakes, I wish the vengeance of G. Britain may speedily overtake their base Deluders. . . . No, believe me, Ned, the Mad Conduct of my Countrymen has given me a Dose I shall never get over— God mend them, & bless them—but let me never, never be cursed with a residence among them again. I hate the Climate where Rebellion and Fanaticism are ingendered —& I would shun it as I would a country infested with the plague—from all which, good Lord, deliver me. I thank you for writing to me, . . .

— Reading No. 5 —

WILLIAM LYON MACKENZIE ON THE SUBJECT OF WILLIAM ALLAN, 1824[5]

This excerpt from Mackenzie's newspaper gives some indication of his methods as a political satirist. William Allan (1770-1853), the subject of the article, was an exceptional example of the many-sided activities of members of the Family Compact. Two years later a group of young Tories threw Mackenzie's printing press into Toronto Harbour.

✓   ✓   ✓

The Favourite of a Governor, or things as they should be

The following very pleasant story was related to me a few days ago, by an acquaintance, on whose veracity I place confidence: A gentleman crossed to York from Oswego; on arriving at the little capital, he enquired for the custom house, as he had some goods aboard to enter at that office—he was shown the place, hard by the quay. The COLLECTOR proved to be a very mild, good-natured gentleman, as might be; quite a man of business too, very conversant with figures; in short, a man well-known on 'Change, as the saying is; he was—Mr. *William Allan.* On opening his trunk, Mr. Z. found some of his letters were to be left at the post-office of York; he enquired where it was located, and in the POST-MASTER, recognized—Mr. *William Allan.* He had some bills which he wished to discount—had them properly endorsed—

[5] *Colonial Advocate,* August 19, 1824.

posted off to the Bank of Upper Canada—was shown the president of that institution, and that PRESIDENT was the indefatigable—Mr. *William Allan.* A day or two after, he was accompanying a friend, who had come to town to pay some money for a store and tavern licence—on arriving at the office of the INSPECTOR of LICENCES, he was amazed to find that functionary also in the person of—Mr. *William Allan.* A review of the militia took place while he stayed—he had the curiosity to go to see it, and recognized in the COLONEL, his (now) old acquaintance —Mr. *William Allan!!* A row took place in the hotel where he lodged; his evidence was wanted, and the acting MAGISTRATE was—Mr. *William Allan!!* Taking up a newspaper to amuse himself, he read the names of the society for strangers in distress—the TREASURER was —Mr. *William Allan!!* Walking with a friend to see the hospital, he was told the names of the TRUSTEES—one of them was—Mr. *William Allan!!* He happened to overhear a debate about a property which had been forfeited, by a man who ran away in the time of the war; the names of the commissioners were mentioned in the course of the argument, and one of them was—Mr. *William Allan!!* Another day he met a friend from Niagara in doleful mood—enquired the cause, and was informed that the COMMISSIONERS *for war losses,* had cut off half his claim—who are the commissioners, asked he of Oswego: the reply was A. B. C. D. and—Mr. *William Allan!!* He sold some of his goods to a merchant, who gave him an order on the treasurer of the district—the TREASURER was—Mr. *William Allan!!* He had occasion to enquire for a black chip hat, and was directed for a good one to apply at the store of Mr. *William Allan!!* He could hold no longer; but amazed, astonished, and confounded, exclaimed, How I pity this poor man, this Mr. William Allan: If he does the duty of so many different situations, his life must surely be a burden to himself; and if he does not, how I pity a country, the laws of which allow one man to hold such a number of important trusts, at one and the same time. Poh! says my uncle Sin. who lives near president Allan, on the same street, you are a stranger and should be silent; you see but a small specimen of the blessings of our provincial government. The

Colonel is an Aberdeensman. An Aberdeensman, quoth I? Yes, says he, a Scotsman, you know. Ah! I have you now—a favourite of the government. Exactly so, was the reply—a townsman of the Hon. and Rev. owner of the palace there, (pointing)—a real man of business, and worth a plum; in short, he is—he is—Mr. *William Allan!!!*

— Reading No. 6 —

EXCERPTS FROM DURHAM'S REPORT, 1839[6]

Lord Durham has been celebrated in English-speaking Canada chiefly for his advocacy of responsible government and reviled in Quebec for his estimate of French Canadians. The report indicates that there was an ample basis for both these opinions about Durham.

✦   ✦   ✦

a. Nature of the Struggle in Lower Canada

In a Despatch which I addressed to Your Majesty's Principal Secretary of State for the Colonies on the 9th of August last, I detailed, with great minuteness, the impressions which had been produced on my mind by the state of things which existed in Lower Canada: I acknowledged that the experience derived from my residence in the Province had completely changed my view of the relative influence of the causes which had been assigned for the existing disorders. I had not, indeed, been brought to believe that the institutions of Lower Canada were less defective than I had originally presumed them to be. From the peculiar circumstances in which I was placed, I was enabled to make such effectual observations as convinced me that there had existed in the constitution of the Province, in the balance of political powers, in the spirit and practice of administration in every department of the Government, defects that were quite sufficient to account for a great degree of mis-

[6] Report on the Affairs of British North America from the Earl of Durham . . . Presented by Her Majesty's Command. Ordered to be printed 11th February, 1839.

management and dissatisfaction. The same observation had also impressed on me the conviction, that, for the peculiar and disastrous dissensions of this Province, there existed a far deeper and far more efficient cause,—a cause which penetrated beneath its political institutions into its social state,—a cause which no reform of constitution or laws, that should leave the elements of society unaltered, could remove; but which must be removed, ere any success could be expected in any attempt to remedy the many evils of this unhappy Province. I expected to find a contest between a government and a people: I found two nations warring in the bosom of a single state: I found a struggle, not of principles, but of races; and I perceived that it would be idle to attempt any amelioration of laws or institutions until we could first succeed in terminating the deadly animosity that now separates the inhabitants of Lower Canada into the hostile divisions of French and English. . . .

The hostility which thus pervades society, was some time growing before it became of prominent importance in the politics of the Province. It was inevitable that such social feelings must end in a deadly political strife. The French regarded with jealousy the influence in politics of a daily increasing body of the strangers, whom they so much disliked and dreaded; the wealthy English were offended at finding that their property gave them no influence over their French dependents, who were acting under the guidance of leaders of their own race; and the farmers and traders of the same race were not long before they began to bear with impatience their utter political nullity in the midst of the majority of a population, whose ignorance they contemned, and whose political views and conduct seemed utterly at variance with their own notions of the principles and practice of self-government. The superior political and practical intelligence of the English cannot be, for a moment, disputed. The great mass of the Canadian population, who cannot read or write, and have found in few of the institutions of their country even the elements of political education, were obviously inferior to the English settlers, of whom a large proportion had received a considerable amount of education, and had been trained in their own country to take a part

in public business of one kind or another. With respect
to the more educated classes, the superiority is not so
general or apparent; indeed from all the information that
I could collect, I incline to think that the greater amount
of refinement, of speculative thought, and of the knowledge that books can give, is, with some brilliant exceptions, to be found among the French. But I have no
hesitation in stating, even more decidedly, that the
circumstances in which the English have been placed in
Lower Canada, acting on their original political education, have endowed the leaders of that population with
much of that practical sagacity, tact, and energy in
politics, in which I must say that the bad institutions of
the Colony have, in my opinion, rendered the leaders of
the French deplorably deficient. . . . Unhappily, however, the system of government pursued in Lower Canada
has been based on the policy of perpetuating that very
separation of the races, and encouraging these very
notions of conflicting nationalities which it ought to have
been the first and chief care of Government to check and
extinguish. From the period of the conquest to the present
time, the conduct of the Government has aggravated the
evil, and the origin of the present extreme disorder may
be found in the institutions by which the character of
the colony was determined.

---

b. *How to Make Government Work*

. . . It is not by weakening, but strengthening the influence of the people on its Government; by confining
within much narrower bounds than those hitherto allotted
to it, and not by extending the interference of the imperial
authorities in the details of colonial affairs, that I believe
that harmony is to be restored, where dissension has so
long prevailed; and a regularity and vigour, hitherto unknown, introduced into the administration of these
Provinces. It needs no change in the principles of government, no invention of a new constitutional theory, to
supply the remedy which would, in my opinion, completely remove the existing political disorders. It needs
but to follow out consistently the principles of the British

constitution and introduce into the Government of these great Colonies those wise provisions, by which alone the working of the representative system can in any country be rendered harmonious and efficient. . . . I would not impair a single prerogative of the Crown; on the contrary, I believe that the interests of the people of these Colonies require the protection of prerogatives, which have not hitherto been exercised. But the Crown, must, on the other hand, submit to the necessary consequences of representative institutions; and if it has to carry on the Government in unison with a representative body, it must consent to carry it on by means of those in whom that representative body has confidence. . . .

The means which have occasionally been proposed in the colonies themselves appear to me by no means calculated to attain the desired end in the best way. These proposals indicate such a want of reliance on the willingness of the Imperial Government to acquiesce in the adoption of a better system, as, if warranted, would render an harmonious adjustment of the different powers of the State utterly hopeless. An elective executive council would not only be utterly inconsistent with monarchical government, but would really, under the nominal authority of the Crown, deprive the community of one of the great advantages of an hereditary monarchy. Every purpose of popular control might be combined with every advantage of vesting the immediate choice of advisers in the Crown, were the Colonial Governor to be instructed to secure the co-operation of the Assembly in his policy by intrusting its administration to such men as could command a majority, and if he were given to understand that he need count on no aid from home in any difference with the Assembly, that should not directly involve the relations between the mother country and the Colony. This change might be effected by a single despatch containing such instructions; or if any legal enactment were requisite, it would only be one that would render it necessary that the official acts of the Governor should be countersigned by some public functionary. This would induce responsibility for every act of the Government, and, as a natural consequence, it would necessitate the substitution of a system of administration, by means of competent heads of departments, for the present rude machinery of an executive council. The Governor, if he wished to retain advisers not possessing the confidence of the existing Assembly, might rely on the effect of an appeal to the people, and, if unsuccessful, he might be coerced by a refusal of supplies, or his advisers might be terrified by the prospect of impeachment. . . . I admit that the system which I propose would, in fact, place the internal government of the colony in the hands of the colonists themselves; and that we should thus leave to them the execution of the laws, of which we have long entrusted the making solely to them. Perfectly aware of the value of our colonial possessions, and strongly impressed with the necessity of maintaining our connexion with them, I know not in what respect it can be desirable that we should interfere with their internal legislation in matters which do not affect their relations with the mother country. The matters which so concern us are very few. The Constitution of the form of government,—the regulation of foreign relations, and of trade with the mother country, the other British Colonies, and foreign nations,—and the disposal of the public lands, are the only points on which the mother country requires a control. . . .

I entertain no doubts as to the national character which must be given to Lower Canada; it must be that of the British Empire; that of the majority of the population of British America; that of the great race which must in the lapse of no long period of time be predominant over the whole North American Continent. Without effecting the change so rapidly or so roughly as to shock the feelings and trample on the welfare of the existing generation, it must henceforth be the first and steady purpose of the British Government to establish an English population, with English laws and language, in this Province, and to trust its government to none but a decidedly English Legislature. . . .

---

c. Inferiority of the French

And is this French-Canadian nationality one which, for the good merely of that people, we ought to strive to perpetuate, even if it were possible? I know of no national distinctions marking and continuing a more hopeless inferiority. The language, the laws, the character of the North American Continent are English; and every race but the English (I apply this to all who speak the English language) appears there in a condition of inferiority. It is to elevate them from that inferiority that I desire to give to the Canadians our English character. I desire it for the sake of the educated classes, whom the distinction of language and manners keeps apart from the great Empire to which they belong. At the best, the fate of the educated and aspiring colonist is, at present, one of little hope, and little activity; but the French Canadian is cast still further into the shade, by a language and habits foreign to those of the Imperial Government. A spirit of exclusion has closed the higher professions on the educated classes of the French Canadians more, perhaps, than was absolutely necessary; but it is impossible for the utmost liberality on the part of the British Government to give an equal position in the general competition of its vast population to those who speak a foreign language. I desire the amalgamation still more for the sake of the humbler classes. Their present state of rude and equal plenty is fast deteriorating under the pressure of population in the narrow limits to which they are confined. If they attempt to better their condition, by extending themselves over the neighbouring country, they will necessarily get more and more mingled with an English population: if they prefer remaining stationary, the greater part of them must be labourers in the employ of English capitalists. In either case it would appear that the great mass of the French Canadians are doomed, in some measure, to occupy an inferior position, and to be dependent on the English for employment. The evils of poverty and dependence would merely be aggravated in a ten-fold degree, by a spirit of jealous and resentful nationality, which should separate the working class of the community from the possessors of wealth and employers of labour. . . .

There can hardly be conceived a nationality more destitute of all that can invigorate and elevate a people, than that which is exhibited by the descendants of the French in Lower Canada, owing to their retaining their peculiar language and manners. They are a people with no history, and no literature. The literature of England is written in a language which is not theirs; and the only literature which their language renders familiar to them, is that of a nation from which they have been separated by eighty years of a foreign rule and still more by those changes which the Revolution and its consequences have wrought in the whole political, moral, and social state of France. Yet it is on a people whom recent history, manners, and modes of thought so entirely separate from them, that the French Canadians are wholly dependent for almost all the instruction and amusement derived from books: it is on this essentially foreign literature, which is conversant about events, opinions, and habits of life, perfectly strange and unintelligible to them, that they are compelled to be dependent. Their newspapers are mostly written by natives of France, who have either come to try their fortunes in the Province, or been brought into it by the party leaders, in order to supply the dearth of literary talent available for the political press. In the same way their nationality operates to deprive them of the enjoyments and civilizing influence of the arts. Though descended from the people in the world that most generally love, and have most successfully cultivated the drama—though living on a continent, in which almost every town, great or small, has an English theatre, the French population of Lower Canada, cut off from every people that speaks its own language, can support no national stage.

In these circumstances, I should be indeed surprised if the more reflecting part of the French Canadians entertained at present any hope of continuing to preserve their nationality. . . .

But the period of gradual transition is past in Lower Canada. In the present state of feeling among the French population, I cannot doubt that any power which they might possess would be used against the policy and the very existence of any form of British government. I cannot doubt that any French Assembly that shall again meet in Lower Canada will use whatever power, be it more or less limited, it may have, to obstruct the Government, and undo whatever has been done by it. Time, and the honest co-operation of the various parties, would be required to aid the action of a federal constitution; and time is not allowed, in the present state of Lower Canada, nor co-operation to be expected from a legislature of which the majority shall represent its French inhabitants. I believe that tranquillity can only be restored by subjecting the Province to the vigorous rule of an English majority; and that the only efficacious government would be that formed by a legislative union.

— Reading No. 7 —

EXCERPT FROM ELGIN'S LETTER TO GREY, MARCH 23, 1850[7]

This correspondence passed between James Bruce, eighth Earl of Elgin (1811-1863) and Henry George, third Earl Grey (1802-1894) during Elgin's tenure of office as Governor-General of British North America. Since the correspondence was private, it gives an admirable inside account of the problems confronting the administration and a vivid picture of the personalities of Grey and Elgin. Elgin protested against a speech by the British Prime Minister, Lord John Russell (1792-1878) on February 8, 1850, in which he suggested that the colonies might eventually become independent. The letter indicates Elgin's fervent love for the Empire and his desire to keep Canada within it.

✔   ✔   ✔

Lord John's speech on the Colonies seems to have been eminently successful at home— It is calculated too I think to do good in the Colonies—but for one sentence, the introduction of which I deeply deplore—the sting in the tail— Alas! for that sting in the tail!— I much fear that when the liberal and enlightened sentiments, the enunciation of which by one so high in authority is so well calculated to make the Colonists sensible of the advantages which they derive from their connexion with Great Britain, shall have passed away from their memories, there will not be wanting those who will remind them that on this solemn occasion the Prime Minister of England amid

[7] *The Elgin-Grey Papers, 1846-1852* (Ottawa, 1937), II, 608-611.

the plaudits of a full Senate declared that he looked forward to the day when the ties which he was endeavouring
to render so easy & mutually advantageous would be
severed! . . . But how does the case stand with us?—no
matter how great the advance of a British Colony in
wealth and civilization—no matter how absolute the
powers of self-government conceded to it—it is still
taught to believe that it is in a condition of pupilage from
which it must pass before it can attain maturity. For one,
I have never been able to comprehend why, elastic as our
constitutional system is, we should not be able, now more
especially when we have ceased to control the trade of
our Colonies, to render the links which bind them to the
British Crown at least as lasting as those which unite the
component parts of the Union— I do not say that the
relation subsisting between the Mother Country and the
Colonies may not have to be in some cases modified—
Here for instance, where the vicinity of the U. S. exercises
so great an influence, it is, I think, possible, that the time
may come when it may be expedient to allow the Colonists to elect their own Governors, to reduce their civil
lists to the starvation point, &c, England withdrawing all
her forces except 2,000 men at Quebec & being herself
represented in the Colony by an Agent—something like
a Resident in India— If yr. agent was well chosen and
had a good status, I am not sure but that the connexion
might be kept up under such an arrangement quite as
well and as profitably for England as under the present—
One thing is however indispensable to the success of this
or any other system of Colonial Govt— You must renounce the habit of telling the Colonies that the Colonial
is a provisional existence.—You must allow them to believe that without severing the bonds which unite them
to Great Britain they may attain the degree of perfection
and of social and political developement to which organized communities of freemen have a right to aspire.—. . .

I may perhaps be expressing myself too un[re]servedly
with reference to opinions emanating from a source which
I am no less disposed than bound to respect— As I have
the means however of feeling the pulse of the Colonists in
this most feverish region I consider it to be always my
duty to furnish you with as faithful a record as possible

of our diagnostics— And after all, may I not with all submission ask, is not the question at issue a most momentous one? What is it indeed but this? Is the Queen of England to be the Sovereign of an Empire, growing, expanding, strengthening itself from age to age—striking its roots deep into fresh earth and drawing new supplies of vitality from virgin soils?—Or is She to be for all essential purposes of might and power monarch of Great Britain and Ireland merely— Her place & that of Her line in the World's History determined by the productiveness of 12,000 square miles of a coal formation which is being rapidly exhausted, and the duration of the social and political organization over which She presides dependant on the annual expatriation with a view to its eventual alienization of the surplus swarm of Her born Subjects? If Lord John Russell instead of concluding his excellent speech with a declaration of opinion which, as I read it and as I fear others will read it, seems to make it a point of honor with the Colonists to prepare for separation,— had contented himself with resuming the statements already made in it's course—with shewing that neither the Govt nor Part could have any object in view in their Colonial Policy but the good of the Colonies, and the establishment of the relation between them and the Mother Country on the basis of mutual affection—that, as the idea of maintaining a Colonial Empire for the purpose of exercising dominion or dispensing patronage had been for some time abandoned, and that of regarding it as a hotbed for forcing Commerce and manufactures more recently renounced, a greater amount of free action and self Government might be conceded to British Colonies without any breach of Imperial Unity or the violation of any principle of Imperial Policy, than had under any scheme yet devised fallen to the lot of the component parts of any Federal or Imperial system—if he had left these great truths to work their effect without hazarding a conjecture, which will I fear be received as a suggestion, with respect to the course which certain wayward members of the Imperial family may be expected to take in a contingency still confessedly remote, it would, I venture with great deference to submit, in so far at least as public feeling in the colonies is concerned, have been safer. . . .

— Reading No. 8 —

VINDICATION OF CANADIAN FISCAL AUTONOMY, 1859[8]

When the Duke of Newcastle, the Colonial Secretary in the Imperial Government, protested against protectionist features of the Canadian tariff, A. T. Galt, the Minister of Finance, replied in vigorous terms.

✓   ✓   ✓

From expressions used by his Grace in reference to the sanction of the Provincial Customs Act, it would appear that he had even entertained the suggestion of its disallowance; and though, happily Her Majesty has not been so advised, yet the question having been thus raised, and the consequences of such a step, if ever adopted, being of the most serious character, it becomes the duty of the Provincial Government distinctly to state what they consider to be the position and rights of the Canadian Legislature.

Respect to the Imperial Government must always dictate the desire to satisfy them that the policy of this country is neither hastily nor unwisely formed; and that due regard is had to the interests of the Mother Country as well as of the Province. But the Government of Canada acting for its Legislature and people cannot, through those feelings of deference which they owe to the Imperial authorities, in any manner waive or diminish the right of the people of Canada to decide for themselves both as to the mode and extent to which taxation shall be imposed. The Provincial Ministry are at all times ready to

[8] Public Archives of Canada, *Series E,* State Book U; Minister of the Executive Council, November 12, 1859, Report of the Minister of Finance, October 25, 1859.

afford explanations in regard to the acts of the Legislature to which they are party; but subject to their duty and allegiance to Her Majesty, their responsibility in all general questions of policy must be to the Provincial Parliament, by whose confidence they administer the affairs of the country; and in the imposition of taxation, it is so plainly necessary that the Administration and the people should be in accord, that the former cannot admit responsibility or require approval beyond that of the local Legislature. Self-government would be utterly annihilated if the views of the Imperial Government were to be preferred to those of the people of Canada. It is, therefore, the duty of the present Government distinctly to affirm the right of the Canadian Legislature to adjust the taxation of the people in the way they deem best, even if it should unfortunately happen to meet the disapproval of the Imperial Ministry. Her Majesty cannot be advised to disallow such acts, unless Her advisers are prepared to assume the administration of the affairs of the Colony irrespective of the views of its inhabitants.

The Imperial Government are not responsible for the debts and engagements of Canada. They do not maintain its judicial, educational, or civil service; they contribute nothing to the internal government of the country, and the Provincial Legislature acting through a ministry directly responsible to it, has to make provision for all these wants; they must necessarily claim and exercise the widest latitude as to the nature and extent of the burthens to be placed upon the industry of the people. The Provincial Government believes that his Grace must share their own convictions on this important subject; but as serious evil would have resulted had his Grace taken a different course, it is wiser to prevent future complication by distinctly stating the position that must be maintained by every Canadian Administration.

These remarks are offered on the general principle of colonial taxation. It is, however, confidently believed, that had his Grace been fully aware of the facts connected with the recent Canada Customs Act, his Despatch would not have been written in its present terms of disapproval.

The Canadian Government are not disposed to assume the obligation of defending their policy against such assailants as the Sheffield Chamber of Commerce; but as his Grace appears to have accepted these statements as correct, it may be well to show how little the memorialists really understood of the subject they have ventured to pronounce upon so emphatically.

— Reading No. 9 —

THE HAZARDS OF TRANSPORTATION IN THE PRE-RAILWAY PERIOD, 1854[9]

T. C. Keefer (1821-1915), a distinguished Canadian civil engineer was employed on the Erie and Welland canals and on the Ottawa and St. Lawrence river works and became one of the leading hydraulic engineers of the continent. He wrote extensively on problems connected with transportation. Here he describes an exciting and recurrent incident in the navigation of the Ottawa River, the ascent of "Les Chenaux" rapids by the good ship, George Buchanan.

✦   ✦   ✦

Few who have ever had the good fortune to make a trip in the "George Buchanan," when the subsiding waters for the first time of the season encouraged her daring skipper to brave the terrible *chute,* can have forgotten the excitement of the scene. As she neared the dreaded channel, the passengers gathered in clusters on the forecastle —the fireman selected his choicest fuel—the engineer screwed up his slackening bolts and greased his ricketty bearings—the captain stood by his bell. By judicious steering and hard paddling the lower current was surmounted, and the little craft glided into the eddy which led up to the very vortex of the rapid; suddenly the engine ceased its revolutions—an ominous silence reigned throughout the boat, as taking advantage of the eddy which bore her

[9] T. C. Keefer, *"Montreal" and "The Ottawa"* (Montreal, 1854), p. 47.

up to the scene of her laurels or her shame, the boiler gathered steam for the approaching contest. The engineer rolls up his sleeves—the fireman pokes the fire—the captain eyes his enemy—and when the friendly eddy is exhausted nervously rings the bell for "full steam." The engineer throws off the eccentric and seizes a lever in each hand—for full steam cannot be depended upon from the wobbling shaft of the crazy eccentric:—as the cylinders are charged, a cloud of steam fills the waist of the boat, looming through which a spectral figure is seen frantically working the steam port valves as if life depended on the result. If the feat is performed and the little boat has secured a safe position above the rapids—the captain comes down from his perch—the fireman pops up through his hatch, and the engineer rushes out from his misty den, when, looking back with grim satisfaction on the vanquished waters, mutual congratulations are exchanged on the forecastle.

— Reading No. 10 —

THE CHURCH OF ENGLAND ON THE FRONTIER, 1848 [10]

Charles Forest, a graduate of Bishop's College, wrote to the principal of Bishop's describing his problems in the parish of Grenville on the north shore of the Ottawa River. His letter indicates the bitterness of the struggle between the religious denominations in a frontier community.

✓   ✓   ✓

On my departure from college you were pleased to express the interest you felt in my future career and to request that I would communicate to you any information of which I might possess myself as to the condition and prospects of the mission in which I might be appointed permanently to serve. Thanking you most cordially for your kind sympathy with me in my labors, I now take the liberty of complying with your request,—regretting, however, that it is not in my power to say much that is commendatory of our *present* condition.

Grenville, as you are well aware, has been from the first, "a condemned Township," rocky and rough in its general feature, having only about one third fit for arable purposes and another third for grazing etc. Its inhabitants have been kept poor and miserable, struggling in vain against poverty and want, so that, at this moment, not above a tithe of the population have attained to anything like a competency or independence. . . .

[10] *Nicolls Papers* (at Bishop's University, Lennoxville), Charles Forest to Jasper Nicolls, Grenville Parsonage, December 30, 1848.

In point of religious persuasion, we have them here of many shades and distinctions. We have first Presbyterians of the old "blue" school, who closely associate the idea of "church" with that of the "fire and brimstone" and who very sagaciouslv determine that St. John must have had an eye to the Church of England when he superadded his "many antichrists," i.e. Bishops, to the great antichrist, ἄναξ ἀνερῶν τε θέων τέ who holds his seat upon "the seven hills." Some of these do sometimes give me a "good day sir"; but others again would "almaist as sune shak hands wi paperie hersel," as be commonly civil to a clergyman of the Church of England. Second. Then we have our diluted Presbyterianism which to a little stickling for "extempore prayer and plain music" adjoins an unfeigned preference for the measure of scriptural teaching which our establishment affords. Fifty or more of this class attend our weekly ministration, and while I carefully guard against anything which can give offence, I occasionally throw in a reason or two for the customs of the English church, by this means undermining, gradually, the remains of prejudice which may still find place among them. Two-thirds of the children in the Sunday School are of Presbyterian parents. They learn the catechism, collects etc. etc., respond in the service, in short, perform their parts precisely as do the children who have been born in and bred to the church. One advantage I have over these, which is not always enjoyed by clergymen of the church. It is this. Mr. Wm Mair, their Minister, although a tolerable preacher, is not a pastor. He never visits . . . them when sick. Now, seeing the vantage ground of the Church, I have studied to set forth the solicitude, not of Charles Forest, but of the Church as "a nursing mother" for all persons thus situated. I visit Presbyterian and Episcopalian without difference, unless it be that to the latter I speak plainly upon all the doctrines of the Church, while in my intercourse with the others I confine myself to the un-controvertible principles of Christian faith. And, I have little doubt but that in a few years almost all these persons will attach themselves to our communion. We had THREE NEW communicants from this class on Christmas Day.

Three. A third class are the *Methodists*. If these sectaries have done mischief elsewhere, beyond all bounds they have done so *here*. They have had emissaries at work, the most ignorant and debased of their kind, men, not only unskilled in every thing which a divine ought to know, but absolutely unable to read the ordinary text of our English bibles without hesitation and spelling. The mischief has been that a religion of *feelings* has been established!—A "feeling well" or "lively" as they express it, has stood in the place of those *convictions and principles* which conduce to faith and obedience of the gospel of Christ.

— Reading No. 11 —

LIFE ON THE UPPER CANADIAN FRONTIER, 1852[11]

Susannah Moodie (1803-1885) was the wife of a half-pay retired officer who settled in the Peterborough area. She wrote a number of books. The best known, Roughing It in the Bush, *gives a picture of frontier life seen through the eyes of a cultured, critical, and very observant settler. In this excerpt Mrs. Moodie describes a logging bee at the Moodie homestead.*

1   1   1

A logging bee followed the burning of the fallow as a matter of course. In the bush, where hands are few and labour commands an enormous rate of wages, these gatherings are considered indispensable, and much has been written in their praise; but to me, they present the most disgusting picture of a bush life. They are noisy, riotous, drunken meetings, often terminating in violent quarrels, sometimes even in bloodshed. Accidents of the most serious nature often occur, and very little work is done when we consider the number of hands employed, and the great consumption of food and liquor.

I am certain, in our case, had we hired with the money expended in providing for the bee, two or three industrious, hard-working men, we should have got through twice as much work, and have had it done well, and have been the gainers in the end.

People in the woods have a craze for giving and going to bees, and run to them with as much eagerness as a

[11] Susannah Moodie, *Roughing It in the Bush* or *Forest Life in Canada* (New edition, Toronto, 1913), pp. 341 ff.

peasant runs to a racecourse or a fair; plenty of strong
drink and excitement making the chief attraction of the
bee.

In raising a house or barn, a bee may be looked upon
as a necessary evil, but these gatherings are generally
conducted in a more orderly manner than those for logging. Fewer hands are required, and they are generally
under the control of the carpenter who puts up the frame,
and if they get drunk during the raising, they are liable
to meet with very serious accidents.

Thirty-two men, gentle and simple, were invited to our
bee, and the maid and I were engaged for two days preceding the important one, in baking and cooking for the
entertainment of our guests. When I looked at the quantity
of food we had prepared, I thought that it never could
be all eaten, even by thirty-two men. It was a burning hot
day towards the end of July when our loggers began to
come in, and the "gee!" and "ha!" to encourage the oxen
resounded on every side. . . .

Our men worked well until dinner-time, when, after
washing in the lake, they all sat down to the rude board
which I had prepared for them, loaded with the best fare
that could be procured in the bush. Pea-soup, legs of pork,
venison, eel, and raspberry pies, garnished with plenty of
potatoes, and whiskey to wash them down, besides a large
iron kettle of tea. To pour out the latter, and dispense it
round, devolved upon me. My brother and his friends,
who were all temperance men, and consequently the best
workers in the field, kept me and the maid actively employed in replenishing their cups.

The dinner passed off tolerably well; some of the lower
order of the Irish settlers were pretty far gone, but they
committed no outrage upon our feelings by either swearing or bad language, a few harmless jokes alone circulat-
ing among them. . . .

After the sun went down, the logging-band came in to
supper, which was all ready for them. Those who remained sober ate the meal in peace, and quietly returned
to their own homes, while the vicious and the drunken
stayed to brawl and fight.

After having placed the supper on the table, I was so
tired with the noise, and heat, and fatigue of the day,

that I went to bed, leaving to Mary and my husband the care of the guests.

The little bed-chamber was only separated from the kitchen by a few thin boards; and, unfortunately for me and the girl, who was soon forced to retreat thither, we could hear all the wickedness and profanity going on in the next room. My husband, disgusted with the scene, soon left it, and retired into the parlour with the few of the loggers who, at that hour, remained sober. The house rang with the sound of unhallowed revelry, profane songs, and blasphemous swearing. It would have been no hard task to have imagined these miserable, degraded beings, fiends instead of men. How glad I was when they at last broke up, and we were once more left in peace to collect the broken glasses and cups, and the scattered fragments of that hateful feast!

We were obliged to endure a second and a third repetition of this odious scene, before sixteen acres of land were rendered fit for the reception of our fall crop of wheat.

My hatred for these tumultuous, disorderly meetings was not in the least decreased by my husband being twice seriously hurt while attending them. After the second injury he received, he seldom went to them himself, but sent his oxen and servant in his place. In these odious gatherings, the sober, moral, and industrious man is more likely to suffer than the drunken and profane, as, during the delirium of drink, these men expose others to danger as well as themselves.

— Reading No. 12 —

QUEBEC SOCIETY IN 1864 AND 1865 [12]

Frances Monck, a sister-in-law of the fourth Viscount Monck (1819-1894), Governor-General of British North America, was a visitor at Spencerwood, the vice-regal residence at Quebec City in 1864-1865. She described Quebec society in the immediate pre-confederation period.

June 8, 1864. . . .

Some of us went to the House of Commons at Quebec. I was a good deal amused for a short time, but we stayed too long (till near eleven), and the debate was not interesting. Col. Gordon took care of us. I had a long talk with nice Mr. Rose. It is wonderful the way the M.P.'s abuse and contradict each other. Sometimes they throw pellets of paper at each other. The speaker looks like a priest with a priest's hat. M. Cartier was introduced to me! That most quaint-looking McGee was also introduced, he looks like a wild Indian. We got home about twelve, it was so hot and stuffy. Canadians hate air.

June 17, 1864: The vice-regal ball. . . .

The verandah was veiled in with a hundred and eighty yards of fine white muslin, nailed down to keep out the mosquitoes and insects, or "bugs," as the Yankees call

[12] Frances E. O. Monck, *My Canadian Leaves* (London, 1891), pp. 29, 37-38, 38-39, 74, 175-177, 244-245, 250-251, 280-281.

them. The 17th band was outside the curtain. The verandah was lit up, and all the soldiers and their lights looked
so very pretty. We assembled in her Ex.'s sitting-room,
and then all walked in in procession. Then the presenta-
tions began, and lasted a few minutes. The dresses were
very good, and a few of the girls nice-looking. They all
bowed *very* low to her Ex., and two people backed out
of the room. I danced all night, and enjoyed myself much.
It was nice walking in the verandah between the dances.
Fan went in to supper with old Sir E. Taché, and Louise
with old M. Cartier. Mr. J. A. Macdonald took me in.
When every one was gone but our own party, Cartier, and
Colonel G., I sang "The Cure," and most of the gentlemen
danced it. Cartier jumped higher than any one.

June 18, 1864. . . .

Cricket again. We looked on, and were well broiled.
I was so giddy from the heat. There was such a look of
Thunder that I would not go in to dinner. Some ministers
dined. We had a pleasant evening, as we sang choruses;
first a Canadian song, and then the Christy Minstrels; I
also sang two solos. M. Cartier sang the solo of the Canadian song. Our choruses sounded very pretty. The G. G.
introduced Mr. Brown to me. He is to become a new minister, and is very nice-looking, tall and greyish, with a
Ponsonby face. M. Cartier is the funniest of little men!

July 21, 1864. . . .

In the evening we sang choruses and played squails.
Mr. Cartier is so funny. He screams and whoops at the
end of some of his Canadian songs. Mr. Cartier and Mr.
S. danced "The Cure," Cartier shouting it at the top of his
voice all the time. Mr. Stanley jumped higher than any one
I ever saw. Mr. Dodwell's face during "The Cure" was a
study, neither exactly laughing nor crying.

*October 15, 1864: Ball for the delegates to the Quebec
Conference on Confederation*

In wind and rain we set off for the ball. We were received by the Ministry in the speaker's room. Some were in grand official uniforms. The G. G. and Mr. Godley looked very nice in theirs. This ball, you know, was given in the Parliament House by the Ministry to the delegates from the Maritime Provinces, who are come here to arrange about a United Kingdom of Canada. The Maritime Provinces mean Nova Scotia, New Brunswick, Newfoundland, and Prince Edward's Island. It was arranged that I was to follow the G. G. with the Prime Minister, Sir E. Taché, and to dance the first quadrille with him, but Sir E. is so very old that he can't dance, and he would not take me in for fear of having to dance with me, so he walked in first alone; then came the G. G., then John A. with me, and then Cartier and Mrs. Godley. "God save the Queen" was played, and we marched up to the throne in procession. Sir R. M. and wife (Gov. of ———) came very late. Between their being late, and old Sir E. hiding behind a screen to escape from me, the first quadrille was upset. The G. G. danced with Madame Cartier, and I with a New Brunswick Minister, Colonel Grey by name. The Ministers were very angry about my being left without my proper partner, and made apologies; but poor Sir E. is about seventy, so I think he was right to hide! I made acquaintance between the dances with Lady M. and with Mrs. Jervoise, who came out here for ten weeks with her husband, and they were nearly lost at sea! She is very pleasing and handsome. Lady M. is also pretty. The G. G. then introduced me to Sir R. M. He asked me to walk about with him and have some refreshments, so off we went. He wore a red riband and order. Well, this old king and I wandered on and on for a long time. A vulgar waiter ran after us and said, "Do you want to go upstairs, sir?" meaning the servants' gallery, upon which my friend waved him off and went on. With difficulty I at last got an ice, and then we lost ourselves quite, and found at last that we were seated under the wrong throne, in the wrong room! This all took up some time, and when we at last found the right room, I danced with Dr. Tupper, Prime Minister of Nova Scotia. The 25th string-band played in one of the rooms; it is a lovely band. When supper was announced, Sir R. M. wanted me again; but it was decreed that Sir E. Taché was to take me. We walked in procession. Sir E. proposed the Queen's health. After supper I danced a quadrille with Sir R. He talked a good deal about "the French element," which, looking at Madame Duval dancing, he said it was delightful to see. He and his wife had been out moose hunting; he said unfortunately he had not shot one animal the ten days he was out. We call Lady M. "La reine Blanche." Captain Seymour came to the ball with us; he was almost the only young man I danced with. Sala was not seen at the ball, though he was said to be there. Sir E. Taché is the only non-dancing old man here—wigs, spectacles, and grey hairs don't hinder people from dancing. We came home early.

January 5, 1865

After lunch yesterday Dick and I went to the rink; he met me in town; we saw some most exquisite skating, Miss M.'s skating is just what Captain W. said of it—"the poetry of motion." I believe he borrowed this expression from Captain Parker, in speaking of a *horse*. She wore red petticoat and stockings, and had a brown dress and pretty fur cap—no cloak, and she looked like one of Leech's pictures; she has lovely fair golden hair. She flies through the rink, and does figures on skates, and bends on one side like a swallow, and she is so perfectly graceful all the time.

January 10, 1865

I drove with Dick after lunch to see the ice-bridge. From Durham Terrace (platform over the river) it has taken beautifully; the paper says it is the best one for years. It looked most curious to see people walking and driving across the river, and skating upon it. Dick had already walked across. . . . We then went to the rink, where the R. A. band was playing, and we saw some exquisite dancing on skates. Captain H. would adore his "muffin" if he could see her on skates. Poor Captain E. was struggling alone on skates, working his arms like a wind-mill, and looking broken-hearted.

February 4, 1865. . . .

After dinner we went to the children's ball at the rink; it was given by the boys of the High school under Mr. Hatch, the clergyman. The boys issued six hundred invites! Mr. Hatch said it taught them how to manage, as they formed a committee and appointed a secretary for the occasion. There was a tremendous crowd. Mr. Hatch stayed with us most of the evening. He introduced the secretary boy to Dick. The boys were so civil, offering food and drink, and flying about on skates with cakes and wine and water. Poor Captain E was almost an illustration of perpetual motion. There he was in red uniform (the only red man there), shuffling round, never stopping; he was like the brook, running on *"for ever."* At last he shot himself up against the wall, which he *held* till he shuffled over to me. He said, "It is not that I *want* to go on so long, but the fact is, I *can't* stop, once I set off; the more I try to stop, the more I go on." He said, "I am taking care of a little girl to-night, but she skates so much better than I do that I need not think of trying to catch her."

— Reading No. 13 —

A QUEBEC WEDDING, 1849[13]

Kate Mountain (1830-1886), the younger daughter of Bishop G. J. Mountain, wrote letters to her sister, Harriet Nicolls in Lennoxville, giving a vivid picture of Quebec life in the period 1847 to 1865. In the following letter she describes the wedding of Eleanor Moore, a maid employed by the Mountain family, to George Keeler, a ship stower. One gets a glimpse of the culture of the poorer people in Quebec.

✓   ✓   ✓

Ellen's wedding was a grand affair at three o clock on Tuesday. She was dressed in her drab merino dress with satin stripes of the same color, given by ma, your shawl, spun silk white with purple satin stripes and a drawn white silk bonnet with a few orange blossoms in her cap and looked very nice. Eliza, as bridesmaid, had a bonnet just like Ellen's, and Jane a blue drawn silk, and a black satin dress and Fanny was done up in sky blue. Eliza Kennedy was there and Ann Hackett and Eliza's sister Mary McGrath and Miss McGrotty. Mrs. Royston done up like a tulip, as well as the children, who had pink rosettes that wouldn't have gone into a soup tureen on their cheeks attached to the ribbon of their hats. John was very smart with pink silk waistcoat, ditto Royston and Richard with his hair parted in the middle and rows of yellow curls at each side, and ditto Steel. And Simpson. . . . Then we were all there and so were the Cochrans and Bell. Capt.

[13] *Nicolls Papers,* Kate Mountain to Harriet Nicolls, April, 1849.

Bradford said he would come, but Armine didn't know what time to tell him.

Afterwards they adjourned to the kitchen, nearly thirty in all, which was decorated with green boughs and carpetted, and a table laid from one end to the other by joining three or four. Keeler is a very respectable-looking man short and stout with reddish hair. They had tea and coffee and chickens and hams and cakes and tarts and buns, and china and silver of all kinds . . . They had wedding cake of three tiers, given by ma, and wine and some soup and separated about half-past ten.

Keeler is a great musician and plays all kinds of instruments. He sang two songs, "The scolding wife," and "Jessy the flower of." Jane sang the "Irish Emigrant" and "the banks of the blue Moselle," which Armine heard and says he has not heard such a beautiful voice in Canada, high, clear and sweet. Richard sang "myself and my bit of a stick" and had to hold a bit of stick in his hand and at the end of every verse twirled himself round and danced and sang which created great amusement. John also sang a song but what it was remains a mystery.

I was carried to and from the chapel.

Ellen's present from Papa was a large table, from Armine a fine green and purple cashmere dress, from me a worktable with blue silk bag and a brown merino, and striped merino dress from mama.

— Reading No. 14 —

A NAME FOR THE DOMINION, 1864[14]

In November, 1864, the Toronto Globe *received a
number of letters suggesting a name for the new confederation. There were many proposals, some more in-
genious than graceful. The names varied from conservative suggestions like the British Confederacy of Canada
to Tupona, made up of the first letters of The United
Provinces of North America, and British Esfiga, from the
first letters of English, Scottish, French, Irish, German,
and Aboriginal. The* Globe *considered the problem in an
editorial entitled* The Name.

✦   ✦   ✦

As most parents know, it is a very difficult thing to find
a name for "baby." Such a multitude of conflicting emotions agitate the soul, such a number of opposite reasons
perplex the mind in favour of this one or the other, that
really but for paramount necessity and the law, it would
be a wonder if babies ever got named by their parents at
all. The chances would certainly be against it, and we
should have a revival of appellations, truthful, forcible,
but not always agreeable, after the fashion of those by
which men in uncivilized societies distinguish separate
personages from each other. We should become inundated
with Messieurs Rednobs, Bowlegs, Squinteyes, Pugnose,
Splayfoots, Fatsides, Thickheads, Longshanks, Straight-
hairs, and Curleywigs; or with Misses Blueeyes, Black-
hairs, Trimancles, Swannecks, Pearleyteeths, Fairbrows,
and Angelshapes. Now, all this would be very disagree-

[14] Toronto *Globe,* November 15, 1864.

able, and therefore we should feel grateful for the trouble
our parents have given themselves, whereby we are saved
from the distress consequent upon having our attention
called to some unpleasant peculiarity in our make every
hour of the day. That trouble was very great. Perhaps
father was matter of fact, and mother very sentimental.
He liked Thomas or Henry, Betsy or Jane, while she liked
Augustus or Theodore, Florentina or Celestina. . . .

But their trouble was nothing to that which we people
of British North America feel, now that we have got to
find a name for our country. The five separate provinces
about to be united by federal bond, are so many parties to
the business. Each one has a right to a voice in the matter,
and each doubtless will have its predilections, just in the
same way as our "papas" and "mammas" or uncles and
aunts. For some time past our columns have been open
to a discussion of the matter, and among Canadians the
diversity of opinion is very great. What will be the differences when the sister colonies join in the controversy?
How many will be added to the list with which we are
already supplied? Shall we adopt the Spanish system, and
christen our bantling by two or three and twenty names
in order to satisfy all, and leave each man within our
bounds and the world outside to call him by just that one
fancy or taste may dictate? If not, what shall we do? Here
is a list to choose from, with which our correspondents
have supplied us:—Britannica, Borelia, Ursalia, Tuponia,
Albertania, Canadia, West Britannia, Champlania, Trans-
atlantia, Transylvania, Alexandrina, Canadensia, Albinora,
Vesperia, Mesopelagia, Albona, Laurentia, Niagarentia,
Victoralia, and Cabotia.

We think there are very few Canadians who would
care to exchange their names for any one of these. It will
be noticed, however, that our correspondents agree in
desiring that the appellation of the country should either
be Latinised by having the ia stuck to the tail of it, or
that it should have a Latin name altogether. Now, why
should this be? We are only too well aware that our
philosophers, whenever they want a new name for a new
substance or anything else, rush to their dictionary, and
extract from it some atrocious compound, which they im-
pose on the world. And a pretty mess they are making of

the language! The ugliest words we are called upon to utter are the invention of these learned people. For our part we most decidedly protest against conferring upon this great country a hybrid name, a bastard compound of old and new. Our language is quite copious enough to supply us with plenty of names, which will bear their meaning on their face, appeal to our historical glories, to our sympathies, to our national feeling, and which will not send us ever now and again back to our dictionaries to ascertain their force. Such a name, for instance, as "Norland," suggested by a correspondent the other day. That is thoroughly national; there is not the smallest particle of a foreign element in it. It speaks of the home of our race; it appeals to that long pre-historic period when our forefathers underwent the training necessary to make of them the great, sea-roving, adventure-loving, conquering men they became. It recognizes the fact that the blood of the British people is that which we boast; and it appeals to the verdict the history of the world has pronounced, that the nearer you get to the equator, the less you get of manly virtues; that in the North have always lived the people best able to take care of themselves—the bravest, the strongest, the freest, the most energetic, and the most resolute. Moreover, it is a massive name, natural and effective; nothing pedantic or frivolous about it. No one would think of making it the name of an ocean steamer; in which view the list we have given above may be of service to the Messrs. Cunard, but, with all respect to our correspondents, to Canadians it can be of none.

But we do not advise the adoption of "Norland" or of any other coined word, because we conceive, first, that the assumption of an arbitrary designation would be useless; and secondly, that as we have now all we want, it would be unnecessary. Let us look to the example of our mother country. Her official title is that of "The United Kingdom of Great Britain and Ireland." But who thinks of calling any one born in the old land a "United Kingdomer"? By the Americans the people are often called British; but more generally in the States, and all the world over besides, the ordinary appellation by which the three kingdoms are known is England. The Irishman may not like his nationality to be thus ignored; the Scotchman may

have a similar objection; and the Englishman may desire
that people would more generally remember that he is
neither Irish nor Scotch; still they cannot get rid of the
fact that, the Union Act or a dozen Union Acts to the
contrary, the world will speak of England as comprising
the whole. The reason is apparent—England is the largest,
the wealthiest, and most populous country of the three;
in her chief city the Parliament meets, there are the Court
and the Throne. Now, we believe that Canada will occupy
much the same position towards the other Provinces as
England occupies towards the sister kingdoms. She is the
larger, the wealthier, and the more populous; she has the
seat of government, the representative of royalty, and the
other emblems of authority in her possession. No matter,
then, with what name the Confederation be baptised, she
will almost certainly give her name to the whole. Just as
surely as the other colonies ally themselves with us, their
people will be called "Canadians." This, indeed, is the
case to a considerable extent already. At home, people
very seldom talk of the Nova Scotians, the New Bruns-
wickers, or the Prince Edward Islanders—they all go by
the name of Canadians; and we have yet to learn that
they have any objection to it.

This, though not a sentimental, is, we think, a common
sense view of the subject. The inevitable relieves us of
our difficulty. As it is useless to strive against it, we had
better accept it. But we would not recommend that official
sanction should be given to this swallowing up of the
individuality of the sister Provinces. It would be unjust
to them, and it would produce great difficulty in practice.
We want one official name for the whole, and what better
can we have than British America? Not British North
America; for there is, strictly speaking, no other British
America than that which we shall possess. It links us, on
the one hand, with the mother country, asserts our nationality, speaks of our origin, and points to our aspira-
tions; while on the other, it tells of our affection for our
own land, and vindicates our right to a name which our
republican neighbours would fain monopolize. We are
every bit as much American as they, and we see no reason
why we should yield the designation up to them. Moreover, it is a national name. It is not arbitrary; it comes as

the logical result of our position. It is not too long for official use, and for common parlance, as we have endeavoured to show, it will not be needed. Still, if it were, "British-American" would be far preferable to "United Kingdomer," so far at least as euphony goes. We think, then, we cannot do better than keep the names we already possess, and at once fall into the ranks of the nations as the British American people.

— Reading No. 15 —

EXCERPTS FROM THE BRITISH NORTH AMERICA ACT, 1867 [15]

We print the preamble and the following clauses which bear on subsequent controversies in Canada: 3, in reference to the name of the country; 91-93, indicating the respective powers of the federal and provincial governments; 133, describing the status of the English and French languages; 146, describing the procedure for the admission of additional colonies or provinces to the dominion.

✓   ✓   ✓

An Act for the Union of Canada, Nova Scotia, and New Brunswick, and the Government thereof; and for Purposes connected therewith. 29th March, 1867.

Whereas the Provinces of Canada, Nova Scotia, and New Brunswick have expressed their Desire to be federally united into One Dominion under the Crown of the United Kingdom of Great Britain and Ireland, with a Constitution similar in Principle to that of the United Kingdom:

And whereas such a Union would conduce to the Welfare of the Provinces and promote the Interests of the British Empire:

And whereas on the Establishment of the Union by Authority of Parliament it is expedient, not only that the Constitution of the Legislative Authority in the Dominion

[15] 30 and 31 Victoria, C. 3. Printed in *British North America Acts and Selected Statutes* (Ottawa, 1948), pp. 61-92.

be provided for, but also that the Nature of the Executive Government therein be declared:

And whereas it is expedient that Provision be made for the eventual admission into the Union of other Parts of British North America:

Be it therefore enacted and declared by the Queen's most Excellent Majesty, by and with the advice and Consent of the Lords Spiritual and Temporal, and Commons, in this present Parliament assembled, and by the Authority of the same, as follows: . . .

————

3. It shall be lawful for the Queen, by and with the Advice of Her Majesty's Most Honourable Privy Council, to declare by Proclamation that, on and after a Day therein appointed, not being more than Six Months after the passing of this Act, the Provinces of Canada, of Nova Scotia, and New Brunswick shall form and be One Dominion under the name of Canada; and on and after that Day those Three Provinces shall form and be One Dominion under that Name accordingly.

————

91. It shall be lawful for the Queen, by and with the Advice and Consent of the Senate and House of Commons, to make Laws for the Peace, Order, and good Government of Canada, in relation to all Matters not coming within the Classes of Subjects by this Act assigned exclusively to the Legislatures of the Provinces; and for greater Certainty, but not so as to restrict the Generality of the foregoing Terms in this Section, it is hereby declared that (notwithstanding anything in this Act) the exclusive Legislative Authority of the Parliament of Canada extends to all Matters coming within the Classes of Subjects next hereinafter enumerated; that is to say,—1. The Public Debt and Property. 2. The Regulation of Trade and Commerce. 3. The raising of Money by any Mode or System of Taxation. 4. The borrowing of Money on the Public Credit. 5. Postal Service. 6. The Census and Statistics. 7. Militia, Military and Naval Service, and Defence. 8. The fixing of and providing for the Salaries and

Allowances of Civil and other Officers of the Government of Canada. 9. Beacons, Buoys, Lighthouses, and Sable Island. 10. Navigation and Shipping. 11. Quarantine and the Establishment and Maintenance of Marine Hospitals. 12. Sea Coast and Inland Fisheries. 13. Ferries between a Province and any British or Foreign Country or between Two Provinces. 14. Currency and Coinage. 15. Banking, Incorporation of Banks, and the Issue of Paper Money. 16. Savings Banks. 17. Weights and Measures. 18. Bills of Exchange and Promissory Notes. 19. Interest. 20. Legal Tender. 21. Bankruptcy and Insolvency. 22. Patents of Invention and Discovery. 23. Copyrights. 24. Indians and Lands reserved for the Indians. 25. Naturalization and Aliens. 26. Marriage and Divorce. 27. The Criminal Law, except the Constitution of Courts of Criminal Jurisdiction, but including the Procedure in Criminal Matters. 28. The Establishment, Maintenance, and Management of Penitentiaries. 29. Such Classes of Subjects as are expressly excepted in the Enumeration of the Classes of Subjects by this Act assigned exclusively to the Legislatures of the Provinces. And any Matter coming within any of the Classes of Subjects enumerated in this Section shall not be deemed to come within the Class of Matters of a local or private Nature comprised in the Enumeration of the Classes of Subjects by this Act assigned exclusively to the Legislatures of the Provinces.

---

92. In each Province the Legislature may exclusively make Laws in relation to Matters coming within the Classes of Subjects next hereinafter enumerated; that is to say,—1. The Amendment from Time to Time, notwithstanding anything in this Act, of the Constitution of the Province, except as regards the Office of Lieutenant-Governor. 2. Direct Taxation within the Province in order to the Raising of a Revenue for Provincial Purposes. 3. The borrowing of Money on the sole Credit of the Province. 4. The Establishment and Tenure of Provincial Offices and the Appointment and Payment of Provincial Officers. 5. The Management and Sale of the Public Lands belonging to the Province and of the Timber and Wood thereon. 6. The Establishment, Maintenance, and Man-

agement of Public and Reformatory Prisons in and for the Province. 7. The Establishment, Maintenance, and Management of Hospitals, Asylums, Charities, and Eleemosynary Institutions in and for the Province, other than Marine Hospitals. 8. Municipal Institutions in the Province. 9. Shop, Saloon, Tavern, Auctioneer, and other Licences in order to the raising of a Revenue for Provincial, Local, or Municipal Purposes. 10. Local Works and Undertakings other than such as are of the following Classes:—a. Lines of Steam or other Ships, Railways, Canals, Telegraphs, and other Works and Undertakings connecting the Province with any other or others of the Provinces, or extending beyond the Limits of the Province: b. Lines of Steam Ships between the Province and any British or Foreign Country: c. Such Works as, although wholly situate within the Province, are before or after their Execution declared by the Parliament of Canada to be for the general Advantage of Canada or for the Advantage of Two or more of the Provinces. 11. The Incorporation of Companies with Provincial Objects. 12. The Solemnization of Marriage in the Province. 13. Property and Civil Rights in the Province. 14. The Administration of Justice in the Province, including the Constitution, Maintenance, and Organization of Provincial Courts, both of Civil and of Criminal Jurisdiction, and including Procedure in Civil Matters in those Courts. 15. The Imposition of Punishment by Fine, Penalty, or Imprisonment for enforcing any Law of the Province made in relation to any Matter coming within any of the Classes of Subjects enumerated in this Section. 16. Generally all Matters of a merely local or private Nature in the Province.

———

93. In and for each Province the Legislature may exclusively make Laws in relation to Education, subject and according to the following Provisions:—1. Nothing in any such Law shall prejudicially affect any Right or Privilege with respect to Denominational Schools which any Class of Persons have by Law in the Province at the Union: 2. All the Powers, Privileges, and Duties at the Union by Law conferred and imposed in Upper Canada

on the Separate Schools and School Trustees of the Queen's Roman Catholic Subjects shall be and the same are hereby extended to the Dissentient Schools of the Queen's Protestant and Roman Catholic Subjects in Quebec; 3. Where in any Province a System of Separate or Dissentient Schools exists by Law at the Union or is thereafter established by the Legislature of the Province, an Appeal shall lie to the Governor-General in Council from any Act or Decision of any Provincial Authority affecting any Right or Privilege of the Protestant or Roman Catholic Minority of the Queen's Subjects in relation to Education: 4. In case any such Provincial Law as from Time to Time seems to the Governor-General in Council requisite for the due Execution of the Provisions of this Section is not made, or in case any Decision of the Governor-General in Council on any Appeal under this Section is not duly executed by the proper Provincial Authority in that Behalf, then and in every such Case, and as far only as the Circumstances of each Case require, the Parliament of Canada may make remedial Laws for the due Execution of the Provisions of this Section and of any Decision of the Governor-General in Council under this Section.

133. Either the English or the French Language may be used by any Person in the Debates of the Houses of the Parliament of Canada and of the Houses of the Legislature of Quebec; and both those Languages shall be used in the respective Records and Journals of those Houses; and either of those Languages may be used by any Person or in any Pleading or Process in or issuing from any Court of Canada established under this Act, and in or from all or any of the Courts of Quebec.

The Acts of the Parliament of Canada and of the Legislature of Quebec shall be printed and published in both those Languages.

146. It shall be lawful for the Queen, by and with the Advice of Her Majesty's Most Honourable Privy Council, on Addresses from the Houses of the Parliament of

Canada, and from the Houses of the respective Legislatures of the Colonies or Provinces of Newfoundland,
Prince Edward Island, and British Columbia, to admit
those Colonies or Provinces, or any of them, into the
Union, and on Address from the Houses of the Parliament
of Canada to admit Rupert's Land and the Northwestern
Territory, or either of them, into the Union, on such
Terms and Conditions in each Case as are in the Addresses expressed and as the Queen thinks fit to approve,
subject to the Provisions of this Act; and the Provisions
of any Order in Council in that Behalf shall have effect
as if they had been enacted by the Parliament of the
United Kingdom of Great Britain and Ireland.

— Reading No. 16 —

LAURIER ON LIBERALISM, JUNE 26, 1877 [16]

This famous speech was delivered at the Academy of Music, Quebec, on the invitation of the Club Canadien. Laurier attempted to distinguish between Canadian Liberalism and continental liberalism with its anti-Catholic tradition. He defined the political role appropriate to the clergy; it was a very controversial issue in Quebec, as elsewhere.

✓   ✓   ✓

For my part, I belong to the Liberal party. If it be wrong to be a Liberal, I accept the reproach; if it be a crime to be Liberal, then I am guilty of it. For my part, I only ask one thing—that we be judged according to our principles. I would be ashamed of our principles, if we were afraid to give expression to them and our cause would not be worth the efforts for its triumph, if the best way to secure that triumph was to conceal its nature. The Liberal party has been for twenty-five years in Opposition and let it remain there for twenty-five years more, if the people has not yet been educated up to accepting its ideas, but let it march proudly with its banners displayed, in the full face of the country!

Before all, however, it is important to come to an understanding upon the meaning, value and bearing of the word "Liberal" and that other word "Conservative." . . .

Both are susceptible of much good, as they are also

[16] Ulric Barthe (ed), *Wilfrid Laurier on the Platform* (Quebec, 1890), pp. 51-80.

of much evil. The Conservative, who defends his country's old institutions, may do much good, as he also may do much evil, if he be obstinate in maintaining abuses, which have become intolerable. The Liberal, who contends against these abuses, and who, after long efforts, succeeds in extirpating them, may be a public benefactor, just as the Liberal who lays a rash hand on hallowed institutions may be a scourge not only for his own country, but for humanity at large.

Certainly, I am far from blaming my adversaries for their convictions, but for my part, as I have already said, I am a Liberal. I am one of those who think that everywhere, in human things, there are abuses to be reformed, new horizons to be opened up, and new forces to be developed.

Moreover, Liberalism seems to me in all respects superior to the other principle. The principle of Liberalism is inherent to the very essence of our nature, to that desire of happiness with which we are all born into the world, which pursues us throughout life and which is never completely gratified on this side of the grave. Our souls are immortal, but our means are limited. We constantly gravitate towards an ideal which we never attain. We dream of good, but we never realize the best. We only reach the goal we have proposed to ourselves, to discover new horizons opening up, which we had not before even suspected. We rush on towards them and those horizons, explored in their turn, reveal to us others which lead us on ever further and further. . . .

What is grander than the history of the great English Liberal party during the present century? On its threshold looms up the figure of Fox, the wise, the generous Fox, defending the cause of the oppressed, wherever there were oppressed to be defended. A little later, comes O'Connell, claiming and obtaining for his co-religionists the rights and privileges of English subjects. He is helped in this work by all the Liberals of the three kingdoms, Grey, Brougham, Russell, Jeffrey and a host of others. Then come, one after the other, the abolition of the ruling oligarchy, the repeal of the corn laws, the extension of the suffrage to the working classes, and, lastly, to crown the whole, the disestablishment of the church of

England as the State religion in Ireland. And note well:
the Liberals, who carried out these successive reforms,
were not recruited from the middle classes only, but some
of their most eminent leaders were recruited from the
peerage of England. I know of no spectacle that reflects
greater honor on humanity than the spectacle of these
peers of England, these rich and powerful nobles, stub-
bornly fighting to eradicate a host of venerable abuses and
sacrificing their privileges with calm enthusiasm to make
life easier and happier for a larger number of their fellow
beings.

It is true that there is in Europe, in France, in Italy
and in Germany, a class of men, who give themselves
the title of Liberals, but who have nothing of the Liberal
about them but the name and who are the most dangerous
of men. These are not Liberals; they are revolutionaries:
in their principles they are so extravagant that they aim
at nothing less than the destruction of modern society.
With these men, we have nothing in common; but it is
the tactic of our adversaries to always assimilate us to
them. Such accusations are beneath our notice and the
only answer we can with dignity give them is to proclaim
our real principles and to so conduct ourselves that our
acts will conform with our principles. . . .

I maintain that there is not one Canadian Liberal who
wants to prevent the clergy from taking part in political
affairs, if they wish to do so.

In the name of what principle, should the friends of
liberty seek to deny to the priest the right to take part
in political affairs? In the name of what principle should
the friends of liberty seek to deny to the priest the right
to have and express political opinions, the right to approve or disapprove public men and their acts and to
instruct the people in what he believes to be their duty?
In the name of what principle, should he not have the
right to say that, if I am elected, religion will be endangered, when I have the right to say that if my adversary is elected, the State will be endangered? Why
should the priest not have the right to say that, if I am
elected, religion will be inevitably destroyed, when I have
the right to say that, if my adversary is elected, the State
will go into bankruptcy? No, let the priest speak and

preach, as he thinks best; such is his right and no Canadian Liberal will dispute that right. . . .

This right, however, is not unlimited. We have no absolute rights amongst us. The rights of each man, in our state of society, end precisely at the point where they encroach upon the rights of others.

The right of interference in politics finishes at the spot where it encroaches on the elector's independence. . . .

It is therefore perfectly legitimate to alter the elector's opinion by argument and all other means of persuasion, but never by intimidation. As a matter of fact, persuasion changes the elector's conviction; . . . the opinion he expresses is his own opinion; but when, by terror, you force him to vote, the opinion he expresses is your opinion; remove the cause of his fear and he will then express another opinion, which is his own.

— Reading No. 17 —

THE ROLE OF THE FRENCH CANADIAN IN CONFEDERATION, 1889

Speeches delivered by Honoré Mercier (1840-1894), the Quebec nationalist and by Sir Wilfrid Laurier indicate two different conceptions of the role of French Canada in confederation.

✓   ✓   ✓

a. *Honoré Mercier, June 24, 1889* [17a]

As the authorized representative of Quebec . . . with the consciousness of the responsibility attached to my words, I declare in the name of all of us that we have remained and shall remain Catholic and French. Love of the religion and of the nationality of our fathers is stamped upon our hearts, and no one, not even the most potent of tyrants, can take this love from us.

This province of Quebec is Catholic and French, and it will remain Catholic and French.

While protesting our respect and even our friendship for the representatives of other races and other religions, while declaring ourselves ready to give them their legitimate part in everything and everywhere, while offering to share with them as brothers the immense territory and the great resources that Providence has put at our disposition; while desiring to live in the most perfect har-

[17a] Mason Wade, *The French Canadians, 1760-1945* (Toronto, The Macmillan Company of Canada, 1956), p. 426. Reprinted by permission of Mr. Wade and the Macmillan Company of Canada.

mony with them in the shadow of England's flag and under the protection of a sovereign dear to all, we solemnly declare that we shall never renounce the rights which are guaranteed to us by the treaties, the law, and the constitution.

These treaties, this law, this constitution give us the right to remain Catholic and French . . . We are now two million and a half French Canadians in America, proud of our past, strong in our present, and confident in our future; we care little for the threats of our enemies . . .

When we vanish, we shall say to the generation called to succeed us: 'We are Catholic and French, and when you, our successors, vanish in your turn, you must say to the generation which will replace you: "We die Catholic and French!" ' This will be our testament and theirs; the supreme last will of an heroic people, transmitted from father to son, from generation to generation, until the end of time.

b. *Sir Wilfrid Laurier at Quebec, June 24, 1889* [17b]

We are French Canadians, but our country is not confined to the territory overshadowed by the citadel of Quebec; our country is Canada, it is the whole of what is covered by the British flag on the American continent, the fertile lands bordered by the Bay of Fundy, the Valley of the St. Lawrence, the region of the Great Lakes, the prairies of the West, the Rocky Mountains, the lands washed by the famous ocean where breezes are said to be as sweet as the breezes of the Mediterranean. Our fellow-countrymen are not only those in whose veins runs the blood of France. They are all those, whatever their race or whatever their language, whom the fortune of war, the chances of fate, or their own choice have brought among us, and who acknowledge the sovereignty of the British Crown. As far as I am concerned, loudly do I proclaim it, those are my fellow-countrymen, I am a Canadian. But I told it elsewhere, and with greater

[17b] Translated by Ulric Barthe, *op. cit.,* pp. 527-528, and, the latter part, by Mason Wade, *op. cit.,* pp. 427-428. The latter part reprinted by permission of Mr. Wade and the Macmillan Company of Canada.

pleasure, I repeat here this evening, among all my fellow-countrymen, the first place in my heart is for those in whose veins runs the blood of my own veins. Yet I do not hesitate to say that the rights of my fellow-countrymen of different origins are as dear to me, as sacred to me, as the rights of my own race, and if it unfortunately happened that they ever were attacked, I would defend them with just as much energy and vigor as the rights of my own race. I say I: should I not say you, we all of us? Yes, we are too much the sons of France, of that generous nation which has so often shed her blood for the defence of the weak, of the oppressed, not to be ever ready to defend the rights of our fellow-countrymen of different nationalities to the same extent as our own. What I claim for us is in equal share of the sun, of justice, of liberty; we have that share and have it amply; and what we claim for ourselves we are anxious to grant to others. I do not want French Canadians to domineer over anyone, nor anyone to domineer over them. Equal justice; equal rights . . . Cannot we believe that in the supreme battle here on the Plains of Abraham, when the fate of arms turned against us, cannot we believe that it entered into the designs of Providence that the two races, enemies up to that time, should henceforth live in peace and harmony? Such was the inspiring cause of Confederation.

— Reading No. 18 —

METHODISM IN WESTERN
CANADA, 1900-1925 [18]

Dr. Riddell was a Methodist ecclesiastical and educational leader in Western Canada. He describes the transition from the older type of Methodism with its emphasis on salvation to the new type which stressed freedom and social justice.

✓   ✓   ✓

In the Protestant Churches the pulpit has exercised a determining influence in stimulating Christian thought, in focussing Christian attention, and in building Christian character. The Methodist Church in this respect followed the tradition of the Reformed Church and made the pulpit the centre. The early Methodists in the Middle West brought to the pulpit strong interpretative powers based on a definite experience coupled with an insistent persuasive appeal. But in the presence of great social and intellectual changes, the instructional and interpretative function come more and more into prominence. The ministers of the Methodist Church had been trained for leadership in the Church in the application of scientific principles in the search for truth. That search was singularly free from authoritarian or creedal dogmatism. Practical Evangelism had a very small place in its programme. The pulpit felt itself not only free to seek and find the truth but as called of God to embark boldly on the search for truth. Having received his appointment to the pas-

[18] J. H. Riddell, *Methodism in the Middle West* (Toronto, Ryerson Press, 1946), pp. 338-339. Reprinted by permission of the Ryerson Press.

toral oversight of a congregation, he felt himself free to proclaim the truth as he discovered it and as he felt its power in his own experience. Taking the Bible as a great treasure house of revealed truth, he sought by the application of approved principles to find further truth regarding God, the world, human destiny and human relations, all of which found a helpful harmony in the processes then evolving in human life. From the close of the nineteenth century and during the first quarter of the twentieth, the prevailing concern of the pulpit centered around the question of man and his relationship to his fellows. The pulpit felt itself called upon to proclaim the truth that God loved the world of men and valued above everything else those sacrifices and services which tended to make men free from the disability of poverty, sickness, sin and social suffering. Consequently, the central theme emphasized such important truths as the Fatherhood of God, the Brotherhood of Man, and a better world where all the obstacles which prevent men from realizing in their personalities likeness to Jesus might be removed. A new earth in which dwelt righteousness, truth, justice and fair play, became the warp and woof of the pulpit message. On the theological tenets of the Christian faith, there appeared to be little unanimity of opinion.

— Reading No. 19 —

SOCIAL CRITICISM IN 1884[19]

The Week, a journal of comment on politics, literature, the drama and music, was published in Toronto in the period between 1883 and 1896 by Goldwin Smith and a group of associates. It published some of the early poetry of Archibald Lampman, Bliss Carman and others. Its articles indicate the maturity of some Canadian literary and social criticism in this period. This excerpt gives a picture of late Victorian society in Canada.

✓   ✓   ✓

In Canada we rather pride ourselves that our social gatherings are full of life; and if in the Old World an air of boredom, assumed or real, is much in vogue, it cannot be said to be the fashionable craze in this Dominion; yet there is, except with our young people, a perceptible lack of enjoyment to those attending our private parties. Now, as with the best directed energies it is impossible to retain, for any great length of time, a youthfulness that leaves the most of us all too soon, this is an unsatisfactory state of affairs, particularly as even with the first flush of youth gone, there remains with us immense capabilities for enjoyment. Entertainers, however, find no difficulty in getting their invitations accepted, which seems a contradiction to the statement that there is a lack of enjoyment to the participants of their gaieties, which, if people will grumble about, they still also will go to. If parents go to look after their fledglings, *passée* girls, to try and prove they are not *passée*, others because the So-and-So's have a fine house, are swells, and *everyone* who is *anyone*

[19] *The Week*, Toronto, May 15, 1884.

is going, there is a hope, however remote with *all*, of
extracting a little enjoyment out of the evening, a hope
very frequently unfulfilled. The fault sometimes lies in
the guests, oftener with the hosts, who having provided
a great supper and thrown open their beautiful rooms feel
that they have done their duty, and leave their guests to
find their own amusement. Now-a-days everyone with
means and taste expends both, in getting together objects
of art, a friendly rivalry existing as to who has the choicest
pictures or bric-a-brac, while the one who at some party
can provide a surprise in the way of a new floral decora-
tion scores the triumph. But though we may have a keen
eye for beautiful objects, some of us have occasionally
wished something else had been provided for our entertainment. Dancing parties are given more frequently than
any others, and to those who at one time desire to pay off
all social debts, are decidedly the most successful. . . .
The customary engagement cards, with all their facilities
for retaining good dancers, securing pleasant *tête-à-têtes*,
and getting rid of undesirable partners, leave little to be
wished for, but to those who cannot "trip it on the light
fantastic toe," to *chaperons* and wall-flowers, "looking-on"
becomes decidedly wearisome. As to the *chaperons*, well,
no one expects them to enjoy themselves, or receive any
attention except it is to be led into the supper-room first;
the wall-flowers are sometimes a source of anxiety, for
they "are young," or supposed to be, and ought to enjoy
themselves. The gentlemen who support the walls and
door-ways are generally considered able to look after
themselves, but to all who do not dance there is a terrible
want of something to do; the men grow moody, and look
it, the ladies who feel the eyes of the world are upon them
wretched—a wretchedness they endeavour to hide under
smiles and fluttering fans. . . .

But if dancing parties are dull to a few, musical ones
are so to the majority. Although music is voted as one of
the most fascinating of the arts, and is yearly being cultivated to a greater extent among us, no parties are so
universally voted failures as "musicals," and as some
people object to dancing, even if possessed of all the
means for entertaining, there seems to be no chance of
their giving any large entertainments but those that do not

entertain. The reasons for these failures are various. It is
not customary and scarcely practicable in our Canadian
cities to obtain (except bands) the services of professional
musicians, while amateur performances do not always re-
pay the listeners. At a large party it is impossible to give
everyone a seat, and walking about is generally the only
occupation for the majority who, unless some one is "singing," are generally seemingly oblivious to any music that
may be going on. In this "walking-about," one of the chief
draw-backs to the amusement of the evening occurs. For
instance, an acquaintance meets a lady, asks her to take
a walk, or to go and look at the conservatory; she con-
sents, and they get on charmingly for a quarter of an hour
or so; then, having exhausted the flowers and conversation
on subjects of mutual interest, one or other or both think
it would be pleasant to talk to some one else, but neither
like to say so; so they probably wander around (if the
crush permits) for another quarter of an hour, each won-
dering how on earth they are going to get rid of the other,
and when at last the suggestion is made, unless great tact
is used, the suggestor finds he or she has wounded the
amour propre of the companion. When they do start on a
search for the lady's friends, they are sure to be scattered
in different places, and a good deal of time is consumed
in the search, very likely to pounce at last on a solitary
couple, who though possibly equally bored with themselves, it looks somewhat of an intrusion to leave a third
person with.

Then there is something to be said in regard to the way
in which the musical part of the entertainment is arranged. The lady of the house usually asks some of her
musical friends beforehand if they will play and sing for
her, so that they can come provided with music; but as
there is no programme, the performers are left in doubt
as to when they will be called on, which is a fruitful
source of disquietude to a nervous person. Then it is a
great trial for a singer to be obliged by a loud commencement of his song to announce to the talking, laughing multitude that he is going to sing, while scarcely less reassur-
ing are the "hushes" of well-meaning friends who are de-
sirous of obtaining silence. The moment it dawns on the
walking, standing, chatting crowd that some one is sing-

ing, politeness requires an instantaneous quiet. No matter if you *are* at the telling point of your best story or making the wittiest remark, at the first pipe of a shrill voice, the check-rein of politeness pulls you up, and demands a sudden halt, for your reluctant ears to be, perhaps, assailed with a jargon of foreign words, or wonderful shakes or trills of a voice pitched half an octave higher than nature arranged the vocal words for. . . . Dinner-parties are becoming more and more popular, and are growing in favour with young people as well as older ones. Their chief drawback is that they are costly and only entertain a few. When the guests are chosen with tact and skill, the *cuisine* good, and the table appointments well arranged, they often prove delightful. . . . One great advantage in the dinner-party is that it does not upset the usual routine of life. The city man dines at or near his usual hour, and gets to bed at a reasonable time—a great essential for the gentlemen of this work-a-day Canada of ours. He has not an extra meal (as in the case of suppers) thrown in to tax the endurance of his digestive powers, and as the number of guests is limited to a few, there is more chance of congeniality among them.

— Reading No. 20 —

STATEMENT OF PRINCIPLES BY THE CO-OPERATIVE COMMON-WEALTH FEDERATION, 1933[20]

The preamble and the opening sections of the so-called Regina Manifesto gives a fair indication of the basic position of the C.C.F. at the outset of its career.

✓   ✓   ✓

The C.C.F. is a federation of organizations whose purpose is the establishment in Canada of a Co-operative Commonwealth in which the principle regulating production, distribution and exchange will be the supplying of human needs and not the making of profits.

We aim to replace the present capitalist system, with its inherent injustice and inhumanity, by a social order from which the domination and exploitation of one class by another will be eliminated, in which economic planning will supersede unregulated private enterprise and competition, and in which genuine democratic self-government, based upon economic equality will be possible. The present order is marked by glaring inequalities of wealth and opportunity, by chaotic waste and instability; and in an age of plenty it condemns the great mass of the people to poverty and insecurity. Power has become more and more concentrated into the hands of a small irresponsible minority of financiers and industrialists and to their predatory interests the majority are habitually sacrificed. When

[20] Co-operative Commonwealth Federation Programme adopted at First National Convention, Regina, Saskatchewan, July, 1933.

private profit is the main stimulus to economic effort, our society oscillates between periods of feverish prosperity in which the main benefits go to speculators and profiteers, and of catastrophic depression, in which the common man's normal state of insecurity and hardship is accentuated. We believe that these evils can be removed only in a planned and socialized economy in which our natural resources and the principle means of production and distribution are owned, controlled, and operated by the people.

The new social order at which we aim is not one in which individuality will be crushed out by a system of regimentation. Nor shall we interfere with cultural rights of racial or religious minorities. What we seek is a proper collective organization of our economic resources such as will make possible a much greater degree of leisure and a much richer individual life for every citizen.

This social and economic transformation can be brought about by political action, through the election of a government inspired by the ideal of a Co-operative Commonwealth and supported by a majority of the people. We do not believe in change by violence. We consider that both the old parties in Canada are the instruments of capitalist interests and cannot serve as agents of social reconstruction, and that whatever the superficial differences between them, they are bound to carry on government in accordance with the dictates of the big business interests who finance them. The C.C.F. aims at political power in order to put an end to this capitalist domination of our political life. It is a democratic movement, a federation of farmer, labor, and socialist organizations, financed by its own members and seeking to achieve its ends solely by constitutional methods. It appeals for support to all who believe that the time has come for a far-reaching reconstruction of our economic and political institutions and who are willing to work together for the carrying out of the following policies:

1. Planning. The establishment of a planned, socialized economic order, in order to make possible the most efficient development of the national resources and the most equitable distribution of the national income.

The first step in this direction will be setting up of a

National Planning Commission consisting of a small body of economists, engineers and statisticians assisted by an appropriate technical staff.

The task of the Commission will be to plan for the production, distribution and exchange of all goods and services necessary to the efficient functioning of the economy; to co-ordinate the activities of the socialized industries; to provide for a satisfactory balance between the producing and consuming power; and to carry on continuous research into all branches of the national economy in order to acquire the detailed information necessary to efficient planning.

The Commission will be responsible to the Cabinet and will work in co-operation with the Managing Boards of the Socialized Industries.

It is now certain that in every industrial country some form of planning will replace the disintegrating capitalist system. The C.C.F. will provide that in Canada the planning shall be done, not by a small group of capitalist magnates in their own interests, but by public servants acting in the public interest and responsible to the people as a whole.

2. Socialization of Finance. Socialization of all financial machinery—banking, currency, credit, and insurance, to make possible the effective control of currency, credit, and prices, and the supplying of new productive equipment for socially desirable purposes.

Planning by itself will be of little use if the public authority has not the power to carry its plans into effect. Such power will require the control of finance and of all those vital industries and services, which, if they remain in private hands, can be used to thwart or corrupt the will of the public authority. Control of finance is the first step in the control of the whole economy. The chartered banks must be socialized and removed from the control of private profit-seeking interests; and the national banking system thus established must have at its head a Central Bank to control the flow of credit and the general price level, and to regulate foreign exchange operations. A National Investment Board must also be set up, working in co-operation with the socialized banking system to mobilize and direct the unused surpluses of production for socially desired purposes as determined by the Planning Commission.

Insurance Companies, which provide one of the main channels for the investment of individual savings and which, under their present competitive organization, charge needlessly high premiums for the social services that they render, must also be socialized.

3. *Social Ownership.* Socialization (Dominion, Provincial, or Municipal) of transportation, communications, electric power, and all other industries and services essential to social planning, and their operation under the general direction of the Planning Commission by competent managements freed from day to day political interference.

Public utilities must be operated for the public benefit and not for the private profit of a small group of owners or financial manipulators. Our natural resources must be developed by the same methods. Such a programme means the continuance and extension of the public ownership enterprises, in which most governments in Canada have already gone some distance. Only by such public ownership, operated on a planned economy, can our main industries be saved from the wasteful competition of the ruinous overdevelopment and overcapitalization which are the inevitable outcome of capitalism. Only in a regime of public ownership and operation will the full benefits accruing from centralized control and mass production be passed on to the consuming public.

Transportation, communications, and electric power must come first in a list of industries to be socialized. Others, such as mining, pulp and paper, and the distribution of milk, bread, coal, and gasoline, in which exploitation, waste, or financial malpractices are particularly prominent must next be brought under social ownership and operation.

In restoring to the community its natural resources and in taking over industrial enterprises from private into public control, we do not propose any policy of outright confiscation. What we desire is the most stable and equitable transition to the Co-operative Commonwealth. It is impossible to decide the policies to be followed in particular cases in an uncertain future, but we insist upon

certain broad principles. . . . In times of war, human
life has been conscripted. Should economic circumstances
call for it, conscription of wealth would be more justifi-
able. We recognize the need for compensation in the case
of individuals and institutions which must receive adequate maintenance during the transitional period before
the planned economy becomes fully operative. But a
C.C.F. government will not play the role of rescuing bank-
rupt private concerns for the benefit of promoters and
of stock and bond holders. It will not pile up a deadweight
burden of unremunerative debt which represents claims
upon the public treasury of a functionless owner class.

THE STATUTE OF WESTMINSTER, 1931 [21]

The Statute was, in a sense, the legal termination of the progress of Canada and the other dominions toward complete autonomy, a process which had been going on since 1846.

✔   ✔   ✔

1. In this Act the expression "Dominion" means any of the following Dominions, that is to say, the Dominion of Canada, the Commonwealth of Australia, the Dominion of New Zealand, the Union of South Africa, the Irish Free State, and Newfoundland.

2. (1) The Colonial Laws Validity Act, 1865, shall not apply to any law made after the commencement of this Act by the Parliament of a Dominion.

(2) No law and no provision of any law made after the commencement of this Act by the Parliament of a Dominion shall be void or inoperative on the ground that it is repugnant to the law of England, or to the provisions of any existing or future Act of Parliament of the United Kingdom, or to any order, rule, or regulation made under any such Act, and the powers of the Parliament of a Dominion shall include the power to repeal or amend any such Act, order, rule or regulation insofar as the same is part of the law of the Dominion.

3. It is hereby declared and enacted that the Parlia-

[21] George V, c. 4. Printed in *British North America Acts and Selected Statutes, 1867-1948* (Ottawa, 1948), pp. 125-130.

ment of a Dominion has full power to make laws having extra-territorial operation.

4. No Act of Parliament of the United Kingdom passed after the commencement of this Act shall extend, or be deemed to extend, to a Dominion as part of the law of that Dominion, unless it is expressly declared in that Act that that Dominion has requested, and consented to, the enactment thereof. . . .

7. (1) Nothing in this Act shall be deemed to apply to the repeal, amendment, or alteration of the British North America Acts, 1867 to 1930, or any order, rule, or regulation made thereunder.

(2) The provisions of section two of this Act shall extend to laws made by any of the Provinces of Canada and to the powers of the legislatures of such Provinces.

(3) The powers conferred by this Act upon the Parliament of Canada or upon the legislatures of the Provinces shall be restricted to the enactment of laws in relation to matters within the competence of the Parliament of Canada or of any of the legislatures of the Provinces respectively.

— Reading No. 22 —

MACKENZIE KING ON THE NATURE OF THE EMPIRE, MAY 11, 1944 [22]

On January 24, 1944, Lord Halifax, then British Ambassador to Washington, made a speech in Toronto, in which he appeared to advocate closer centralization of the empire. The speech resulted in a storm of protest in Canada. Mr. King's speech to a joint session of the British Parliament on May 11, 1944 was a virtual reply to Lord Halifax. Mr. King advocated a laissez-faire, *decentralized empire.*

✦   ✦   ✦

So long as Britain continues to maintain the spirit of freedom, and to defend the freedom of other nations, she need never doubt her own pre-eminence throughout the world. So long as Britain continues to share that spirit with the other nations of the commonwealth, she need never fear for the strength or unity of the commonwealth.

The voluntary decisions by Britain, by Canada, by Australia, by New Zealand, and by South Africa are a supreme evidence of the unifying force of freedom. This common effort springing from a common source has given a new strength and unity, a new meaning and significance to the British Commonwealth.

Without attempting to distinguish between the terms "British Empire" and "British Commonwealth," but looking rather to the evolution of this association of free nations, may I give to you what I believe to be the secret of

[22] *Winnipeg Free Press,* May 11, 1944.

its strength and of its unity, and the vision which I cherish of its future?

Model of What World May One Day Become

"We, who look forward to larger brotherhoods and more exact standards of social justice, value and cherish the British Empire because it represents, more than any other similar organization has ever represented, the peaceful co-operation of all sorts of men in all sorts of countries, and because we think it is, in that respect at least, a model of what we hope the whole world will some day become."

This vision, I need scarcely say, is not mine alone; indeed, the words in which I have sought to portray it are not even my own. They were spoken thirty-seven years ago by one whose fame today is not surpassed in any part of the world, if, indeed, it has been equalled at any time in the world's history. They are the words of the present prime minister of Britain, uttered by Mr. Churchill in 1907. As they continue to reverberate down the years, they bring fresh inspiration to all who owe allegiance to the crown, and increasing hope to mankind. Visions of youth, sometimes, "Die away, and fade into the light of common day."

Has Not Been So

They fade not because the vision is ever wholly lost, but because resolution wavers, because determination fails, because of seemingly insuperable obstacles. It has not been so with Mr. Churchill. He has not to ask:

"Whither is fled the visionary gleam? Where is it now, the glory and the dream?"

The glory and the dream: Are not they being realized at this very hour, in the strength and unity of the nations of the commonwealth?

From time to time, it is suggested that we should seek new methods of communication and consultation. It is true we have not, sitting in London continuously, a visible imperial war cabinet or council. But we have, what is much more important, though invisible, a continuing conference of the cabinets of the commonwealth. It is a conference of cabinets which deals, from day to day, not infrequently, from hour to hour, with policies of common concern.

When decisions are taken, they are not the decisions of prime ministers, or other individual ministers, meeting apart from their own colleagues, and away from their own countries, they are decisions reached after mature consideration by all members of the cabinet of each country, with a full consciousness of their immediate responsibility to their respective parliaments.

Believes Very Strongly In Close Co-operation

I believe very strongly in close consultation, close co-operation, and effective co-ordination of policies. What more effective means of co-operation could have been found than those which, despite all the handicaps of war, have worked with such complete success? Let us, by all means, seek to improve where we can. We cannot be too careful to see that, to our own peoples, the new methods will not appear as an attempt to limit their freedom of decision or, to peoples outside the commonwealth, as an attempt to establish a separate bloc. Let us beware lest in changing the form, we lose the substance; or, for appearance's sake, sacrifice reality. I am told that, somewhere, over the grave of one who did not know when he was well off, there is the following epitaph: "I was well; I wanted to be better; and here I am."

In the passage I quoted from Mr. Churchill a moment ago, I gave only a part of what he said. He set forth as well the means of realizing his vision of peaceful co-operation.

"Let us," he said, "seek to impress, year after year, upon the British Empire, an inclusive and not exclusive character."

Commonwealth Spirit

Like the nations of which it is composed, the British Commonwealth has within itself a spirit which is not exclusive, but the opposite of exclusive. Therein lies its strength. That spirit expressed itself in co-operation. Therein lies the secret of its unity. Co-operation is capable of indefinite expansion. Therein lies the hope of the future.

It is of the utmost importance to the commonwealth that there should continue to be the greatest possible co-operation among its members. In like manner, it is, I believe, of the utmost importance to the future of mankind that, after the war, there should be the greatest possible co-operation among the nations of the world.

The wartime co-operation of the commonwealth is not the product of formal institutional unity; it is the result of agreement upon policies of benefit to all. Moreover, they are policies that make an appeal "to all sorts of men in all sorts of countries," provided only they are men of good will.

Policies Which Can Be Shared With Other Nations

If, at the close of hostilities, the strength and unity of the commonwealth are to be maintained, those ends will be achieved not by policies which are exclusive, but by policies which can be shared with other nations. I am firmly convinced that the way to maintain the unity of the commonwealth is to base that unity upon principles which can be extended to all nations. I am equally sure that the only way to maintain world unity is to base it upon principles that can be universally applied. The war has surely convinced all nations, from the smallest to the greatest, that there is no national security to be found in the isolation of any nation or group of nations. The future security of peace-loving nations will depend upon the extent and effectiveness of international co-operation.

— Reading No. 23 —

HON. L. B. PEARSON AND CANADIAN FOREIGN POLICY, 1955-1956

The most important exponent of Canadian foreign policy from 1948 to 1957 was L. B. Pearson, the Secretary of State for External Affairs. Pearson played a prominent part in the discussions in the United Nations Assembly after the invasion of Egypt by Israeli, British, and French forces in October and November of 1956. Pearson's proposal for the despatch of a United Nations expeditionary force to Egypt was eventually adopted. It was largely responsible for the termination of hostilities.

✓   ✓   ✓

a. *Canadian Attitude toward the United Nations*[23a]

If we examine the position of the United Nations today, there is of course one obvious and tragic difference from that of 1945. Any unity and understanding between the Big Powers has been lost. As the organization, and in particular the Security Council, was based on the assumption that it would be retained, the repercussions were bound to be far-reaching. The problem of assessing the position of the United Nations in 1955 is, therefore, one of examining to what extent these Big Power differences and misunderstandings have crippled its operations, and whether alternative arrangements might have been or may yet prove feasible. . . .

Even though the United Nations meetings did not always result in agreement or develop satisfactory compro-

[23a] Information Division, Department of External Affairs, Ottawa, *Statements and Speeches* No. 55/23. An address by Hon. L. B. Pearson, San Francisco, June 22, 1955.

mise formulae, I am convinced that the debates in the Assembly have, on the whole, served a useful purpose and have contributed to the maintenance of peace. The United Nations, to some extent at least, has brought the democratic process—and the pressure of public opinion—to bear in the handling of international issues; even on those totalitarian states which have been successful in isolating their peoples from contacts with others and from the direct impact of United Nations discussions. . . .

On the whole, therefore, as I see the organization today, though it is not now the strong agency for general collective security we all visualized in 1945, it has become a useful and potentially effective instrument for that purpose. Both directly and indirectly, it has served the purposes for which it was originally set up, though it has fallen short of the initial objectives we had in mind. Handicapped as it was by the failure of the basic assumption, on which we acted at San Francisco—Great Power co-operation—it has nevertheless facilitated the development of security arrangements which make the prospects of aggression increasingly less inviting.

b. *Canadian Attitude toward the North Atlantic Treaty Organization*[23b]

While I have mentioned the Geneva conference and NATO I would not want to overlook one other useful meeting in recent weeks, the meeting at San Francisco to celebrate the tenth anniversary of the United Nations. I think that meeting turned out to be a very good and valuable development because it focused, and there was need to focus at this time, the attention of the world on the United Nations and its achievements, about which we do not always hear so much, as well as its failures, about which we always hear more; about its limitations as well as its possibilities.

The words used most often in the 72 speeches to which we listened at the San Francisco conference—71 in my case—because I made one myself—were "stocktaking" and "rededication." We took stock of the past and we

[23b] Speech by Hon. L. B. Pearson, *Canadian House of Commons Debates*, July 23, 1955.

looked to the future. Practically without exception, and this also applies to the delegations from the other side of the Iron Curtain, every statement ended with an expression of support for the United Nations as the indispensable and universal agency for the solution of disputes and the removal of difficulties, as the indispensable agency for international co-operation.

If it could only do the work it was meant to do ten years ago when we set it up, we would not be talking today about NATO or conferences at the summit, because we would not need them. It may be that one day we will be able to use that world organization as it was meant to be used. Until that time we will be well advised, insofar as political collective security is concerned, to continue our support for regional organizations like the North Atlantic Treaty Organization, to keep them strong and united, to do our very best to convince those who fear these organizations that they are defensive in character, that they have no aggressive intent against anybody. If conditions improve, if there is more trust and confidence in the world than unfortunately is now the case, then, but only then, we will be able to modify our attitude toward these regional defensive collective organizations, especially if the work which they now do can be done through the United Nations.

c. *Canadian Proposal in Regard to the Middle East Crisis, November, 1956* [23c]

The immediate purpose of our meeting tonight is to bring about as soon as possible a cease fire and a withdrawal of forces, in the area which we are considering, from contact and from conflict with each other. Our longer range purpose, which has already been referred to tonight and which may ultimately, in its implications, be even more important, is to find solutions for the problems which, because we have left them unsolved over the years, have finally exploded into this fighting and conflict.

In regard to this longer range purpose, important reso-

[23c] Department of External Affairs, Ottawa, *Statements and Speeches* No. 56/23, Statement by L. B. Pearson to the Second Meeting of the Emergency Special Session of the U. N. General Assembly, New York, November 3, 1956.

lutions have been submitted this evening by the United States delegation. We value this initiative, and our delegation will give the resolutions the examination which their importance deserves and will, I hope, make its own detailed comments concerning them later.

So far as the first and immediate purpose is concerned, a short time ago the Assembly passed, by a very large majority, a resolution which is now a recommendation of the United Nations General Assembly. And so we must ask ourselves how the United Nations can assist in securing compliance with the terms of that resolution from those who are most immediately concerned and whose compliance is essential if that resolution is to be carried out.

How can we get from them the support and co-operation which is required, and how can we do this quickly?

The representative of India has just read to us, on behalf of a number of delegations, a very important resolution which deals with this matter. In operative paragraphs 2 and 3 of that resolution, certain specific proposals are made with a view to setting up machinery to facilitate compliance with the resolution.

I ask myself the question whether that machinery is adequate for the complicated and difficult task which is before us. I am not in any way opposing this resolution which we have just heard read. I appreciate its importance and the spirit in which it has been put forward. But I do suggest that the Secretary-General be given another and supplementary—not conflicting, but supplementary—responsibility: to work out at once a plan for an international force to bring about and supervise the cease fire visualized in the Assembly resolution which has already been passed.

For that purpose my delegation would like to submit to the Assembly a very short draft resolution which I venture to read at this time. It is as follows:

"The General Assembly, bearing in mind the urgent necessity of facilitating compliance with the Resolution (A/3256) of November 2, requests, as a matter of priority, the Secretary-General to submit to it within forty-eight hours a plan for the setting up, with the consent of the nations concerned, of an emergency international United

Nations force to secure and supervise the cessation of hostilities in accordance with the terms of the above resolution."

I would assume that during this short period the Secretary-General would get into touch with, and endeavour to secure co-operation in the carrying out of the earlier resolution from, the parties immediately concerned —whose co-operation, I venture to repeat, is essential—as well as endeavouring to secure help and co-operation from any others whom he thinks might assist in his vitally important task.

This draft resolution which I have just read out, and which will be circulated shortly, has an added purpose of facilitating and making effective compliance with the resolution which we have already passed on the part of those whose compliance is absolutely essential.

It has also the purpose of providing for international supervision of that compliance through the United Nations, and, finally, it has as its purpose the bringing to an end of the fighting and bloodshed at once, even while the Secretary-General is examining this question and reporting back in forty-eight hours.

If this draft resolution commended itself to the General Assembly—and I suggest that it is not in conflict with the draft resolution which has just been read to us by our Indian colleague—and if it were accepted and accepted quickly the Secretary-General could at once begin the important task which the draft resolution gives him.

I apologize for adding to his burdens in this way, because they have already been added to in the immediately preceding draft resolution, but we know that he can carry burdens of this kind both unselfishly and efficiently.

Meanwhile, during this period of forty-eight hours, we can get on with our consideration of and decision on the United States draft resolution and other draft resolutions before the General Assembly which deal with this grave and dangerous situation which confronts us, both in relation to its immediate as well as its wider and perhaps even more far-reaching aspects.

— Reading No. 24 —

AN ELECTION MEETING, 1957[24]

The revolt of western farmers against the Liberals was a feature of the 1957 election campaign. When the Right Hon. C. D. Howe addressed a Liberal rally at Morris, Manitoba on May 18, 1957, he discovered that the revolt had penetrated the Liberal party itself. The story in the Winnipeg Free Press *gives a picture of vigorous western Canadian politics.*

✓   ✓   ✓

Surplus-suffering Manitoba farmers Saturday night pounced on the man who is responsible for selling Canada's grain crop, turning a carefully planned Liberal rally into a pandemonium of shouts, jeers and raucous booing.

The place was the crowded auditorium of the Morris High School and the man was Canada's minister of trade and commerce, minister of defence production and deputy prime minister, Right Honorable Clarence Decatur Howe.

The trade minister's presence set the farmers into a turmoil of hoots and hollers like those that came from the little man halfway down the hall who kept jumping up to say, "I've been a Liberal all my life, Mr. Howe!"

But when it was over, he was shouting, "I've been a Liberal up to now, Mr. Howe!"

Local Liberals said that Mr. Howe had defied their advice and determined to sally forth into the teeth of farm unrest in the grain country.

But before he had left the Morris auditorium, the teeth had clamped down hard upon him and he had to battle his way off the platform, shouting over choruses of cat-calls and jeers that he was wanted back in Ottawa.

And back to Ottawa he flew Sunday morning, behind him the rowdiest Manitoba meeting of the election campaign and some of its worst fiascos.

There was, for instance, the man who elbowed his way to the front of the hall at the height of the uproar and asked the chairman if he might not speak from the platform.

Mr. Howe didn't wait for the chairman's reply. He did the replying himself. No, the intruder could not have the platform. "When your party organizes a meeting, you'll have the platform then and we'll ask the questions" said the minister of trade and commerce.

"Well," observed the man from the floor his arms folded jauntily across his chest, "I AM the president of the Liberal association for the constituency of Morris."

"But why," began the trade minister over the howls of the crowd, "but why aren't you up here?"

"I don't know," retorted Bruce MacKenzie, who IS the president of the Morris provincial Liberal association.

There was considerable shuffling and clearing of throats on the platform as Mr. MacKenzie was welcomed to it, patted affectionately on the shoulder by the minister of trade and commerce and escorted triumphantly to the microphone.

But the worst was yet to come. No sooner did Mr. MacKenzie receive the instrument into his hand than he used it to launch into an aggressive attack on:

A. The federal government.
B. Its handling of the wheat problem.
C. Mr. C. D. Howe.

In fact, he began with a little joke, the main point of which was that Mr. Howe had once sat between two provincial premiers as meat between the bread of a sandwich, and that somebody had said it must have been a "baloney" sandwich.

It was at this moment that Mr. Howe discovered the hour was getting late, and he had pressing business back in Ottawa.

A hurried conference was called behind Mr. MacKenzie's back on the platform in an apparent attempt to deal with the problem of getting Mr. MacKenzie away from the microphone and back into the crowd.

As the conference huddled, they cast anxious glances over their shoulders to hear what Mr. MacKenzie was doing to their meeting in language vigorous and bold.

The farmers had been told if they gave the government control of wheat sales, they'd have "an orderly market and social security."

"We haven't got them!" (Loud applause).

Mr Howe had been "sliding around the main issue." (Cheers). . . .

The chairman called for somebody to play God Save the Queen. When nobody would, he led the singing himself. And Mr. Howe hurried to the Fort Garry hotel in Winnipeg, where he spent the night before keeping the Ottawa engagement.

— Reading No. 25 —

HON. L. B. PEARSON'S NOBEL PEACE PRIZE LECTURE, DECEMBER 11, 1957 [25]

The award of the Nobel Peace Prize to Hon. L. B. Pearson in 1957 was a signal recognition of Canada's increasing importance in world politics. Mr. Pearson's Nobel Peace Prize Lecture was delivered at Oslo on December 11, 1957. It was a striking exposition of the Canadian viewpoint in regard to the problem of world peace. Mr. Pearson said in part:—

✓   ✓   ✓

There has been more talk of peace since 1945 than, I should think, at any other time in history. At least we hear more and read more about it, because man's words, for good or ill, can now so easily reach the millions.

Very often the words are good and even inspiring; the embodiment of our hopes and our prayers for peace. But while we all pray for peace we do not always, as free citizens, support the policies that make for peace; or reject those which do not. We want our own kind of peace, brought about in our own way.

The choice, however, is as clear now for nations as it was once for the individual: peace or extinction. The life of states cannot, any more than the life of individuals, be conditioned by the force and the will of a unit, however powerful, but by the consensus of a group, which must one day include all states. Today the predatory state, or the predatory group of states, with power of total destruc-

[25] *The New York Times*, December 12, 1957.

177

tion, is no more to be tolerated than the predatory individual.

I wish to look at the problem in four of its aspects—my "Four Faces of Peace." There is peace and trade; peace and power; peace and policy, or diplomacy; peace and people.

One face of peace is reflected in the trade of nations. This is a subject on which thought has changed greatly within the memories of most of us and is now, I submit, in process of rapid further change.

To the philosophers of the nineteenth century it seemed that there must be a motive of real self-interest, of personal gain, that led nations into conflict. To some extent there was.

We know now that in modern warfare, fought on any considerable scale, there can be no possible economic gain for any side. Win or lose, there is nothing but waste and destruction.

Men may not now go to war for trade, but lack of trade may help to breed the conditions in which men do go to war. The connection is not simple.

Rich nations are not necessarily more peace-loving than poorer nations. But poverty and distress—especially with the awakening of the submerged millions of Asia and Africa—make the risks of war greater.

Until the last great war, a general expectation of material improvement was an idea peculiar to Western man. Now war and its aftermath have made economic and social progress a political imperative in every quarter of the globe. If we ignore this, there will be no peace.

The scientific and technological discoveries that have made war so infinitely more terrible for us are part of the same process that has knit us all so much more closely together. Our modern phrase for this is interdependence.

In this sphere our postwar record is better than it is fashionable to recognize. Under the General Agreement on Tariffs and Trade there has been real progress in reducing trade barriers and in civilizing the commercial policies of national Governments. The achievement so far has its limits, of course, and there have been setbacks, but there has been more progress, and over a wider area, than any of us would have dared to predict with confidence twelve years ago.

Now the European nations are launching themselves, through the common market and its associated free trade area, on an adventure in the economic unification of peoples that a few years ago would have seemed completely visionary. Is it any more visionary to foresee a further extension of this co-operative economic pattern? Is it not time to begin to think in terms of an economic interdependence that would bridge the Atlantic; that would at least break down the barrier between dollar and non-dollar countries which, next only to Iron Curtains, has hitherto most sharply divided our postwar One World?

We must have rising living standards in which all nations are participating to such a degree that existing inequalities in the international division of wealth are, at least, not increased.

I now come to peace and power.

Every state has not only the right, but the duty, to make adequate provisions for its own defence in the way it thinks best, providing it does not do so at the expense of any other state.

The economic burden of armaments is now almost overpowering, and where public opinion can bring itself effectively to bear on government, the pressure is nearly always for the greatest possible amount of butter and the fewest possible number of guns.

Nevertheless, defence by power as a first obligation on a state has to be considered in relation to other things than economics. For one thing—and this is certainly true of smaller countries—such power, unless it is combined with the defence forces of other friendly countries, is likely to be futile, both for protection and for prevention; or for deterrence, as we call it. This in its turn leads to coalitions and associations of states.

These may be necessary in the world in which we live but they do extend the area of a possible war, in the hope that greater and united power will prevent any war. When they are purely defensive in character, such coalitions can make for peace by removing the temptation of easy victory. But they can never be more than a second-best substitute for the great Coalition of the whole United Nations; established to preserve the peace, but now too often merely the battleground of the "cold war."

Furthermore, the force which you and your allies collect for your own security can, in a bad international climate, increase, or seem to increase, someone else's insecurity. A vicious chain reaction begins.

These coalitions for collective defence are limited in area and exclusive in character. And they provoke counter-coalitions. Today, for instance, we have now reached the point where two—and only two—great agglomerations of power face each other in fear and hostility, and the world wonders what will happen.

If the United Nations were effective as a security agency—which it is not—these more limited arrangements would be unnecessary and, therefore, undesirable.

Certainly the idea of an international police force effective against a big disturber of the peace seems today unrealizable to the point of absurdity. We did, however, take at least a step in the direction of putting international force behind an international decision a year ago in the Suez crisis.

We made at least a beginning then. If, on that foundation, we do not build something more permanent and stronger, we will once again have ignored realities, rejected opportunities and betrayed our trust. Will we never learn?

The stark and inescapable fact is that today we cannot defend our society by war since total war is total destruction, and if war is used as an instrument of policy, eventually we will have total war. Therefore, the best defence of peace is not power, but the removal of the causes of war, and international agreements which will put peace on a stronger foundation than the terror of destruction.

Power, the third face of peace, therefore, is policy and diplomacy. If we could internationally display on this front some of the imagination and initiative, determination and sacrifice, that we show in respect of defense planning and development, the outlook would be more hopeful than it is. The grim fact, however, is that we prepare for war like precocious giants and for peace like retarded pygmies.

Our policy and diplomacy—as the two sides in the "cold war" face each other—is becoming as rigid and defensive as the trench warfare of forty years ago, when two sides dug in, dug deeper and lived in their ditches.

It is essential that we avoid this kind of dangerous stalemate in international policy today. The main responsibility for this purpose rests with the two great world powers, the United States and the U.S.S.R. No progress will be made if one side merely shouts "co-existence"— a sterile and negative concept—and "parleys at the summit," while the other replies "no appeasement"; "no negotiation without proper proof of good faith."

What is needed is a new and vigorous determination to use every technique of discussion and negotiation that may be available; or, more important, that can be made available, for the solution of the tangled, frightening problems that divide today, in fear and hostility, the two power blocs and thereby endanger peace. We must keep on trying to solve problems, one by one, stage by stage, if not on the basis of confidence and cooperation, at least on one of mutual toleration and self-interest.

What I plead for is no spectacular meeting of a Big Two or a Big Three or a Big Four at the summit, where the footing is precarious and the winds blow hard, but for frank, serious, and complete exchanges of views— especially between Moscow and Washington—through diplomatic and political channels.

Essential to the success of any such exchanges is the recognition by the West that there are certain issues such as the unification of Germany and the stabilization of the Middle East which are not likely to be settled in any satisfactory way without the participation of the U.S.S.R. Where that country has a legitimate security interest in an area or a problem, that must be taken into account.

It is also essential that the Soviet Union, in its turn, recognize the right of people to choose their own form of government without interference from outside forces or subversive domestic forces encouraged and assisted from outside.

A diplomatic approach of this kind involves, as I well know, baffling complexities, difficulties and even risks.

Nevertheless the greater these are, the stronger should be
the resolve and the effort, by both sides, and in direct
discussions, to identify and expose them as the first step
in their possible removal.

Perhaps a diplomatic effort of this kind would not succeed. I have no illusions about its complexity or even its
risks. Speaking as a North American, I merely state that
we should be sure that the responsibility for any such
failure is not ours. The first failure would be to refuse
to make the attempt.

The time has come for us to make a move, not only
from strength, but from wisdom and from confidence in
ourselves, to concentrate on the possibilities of agreement,
rather than on the disagreements and failures, the evils
and wrongs, of the past.

It would be folly to expect quick, easy, or total solutions. It would be folly also to expect hostility and fears
suddenly to vanish. But it is equal, or even greater folly
to do nothing; to sit back, answer missile with missile,
insult with insult, ban with ban.

That would be the complete bankruptcy of policy and
diplomacy, and it would not make for peace.

It has too often been too easy for rulers and governments to incite man to war. Indeed, when people have
been free to express their views, they have as often
condemned their governments for being too peaceful as
for being too belligerent.

Perhaps this has all changed now. Surely the glamour
has gone out of war. The thin but heroic red line of the
nineteenth century is now the production line. The war-
rior is the man with a test tube or the one who pushes
the nuclear button. This should have a salutary effect on
man's emotions. A realization of the consequences that
must follow, if and when he does push the button, should
have a salutary effect also on his reason.

I realize that contact can mean friction as well as
friendship; that ignorance can be benevolent, and isolation
pacific. But I can find nothing to say for keeping one
people malevolently misinformed about others. More contact and freer communication can help to correct this
situation. To encourage it—or at least to permit it—is an

acid test for the sincerity of protestations for better relations between peoples.

I believe myself that the Russian people—to cite one example—wish for peace. I believe also that many of them think that Americans are threatening them with war; that they are in danger of attack. So might I, if I had as little chance to get objective and balanced information about what is going on in the United States. Similarly, our Western fears of the Soviet Union have been partly based on a lack of understanding or of information about the people of that country.

Misunderstanding of this kind, arising from ignorance, breeds fear, and fear remains the greatest enemy of peace.

A common fear, however, which usually means a common foe, is also, regrettably, the strongest force bringing people together; but in opposition to something or someone. Perhaps there is a hopeful possibility here in the conquest of outer space. Interplanetary activity may give us planetary peace. Once we discover Martian space ships hovering over earth's airspace, we will come together. "How dare they threaten us like this," we shall shout, as one, at a really United Nations!

Even people with generous and understanding hearts and peaceful instincts in their normal and individual behaviour, can become fighting and even savage national animals under the incitements of collective emotion. Why this happens is the core of our problem of peace and war.

That problem, why men fight who aren't necessarily fighting men, was posed for me in a new and dramatic way one Christmas Eve in London during World War II. The air raid sirens had given their grim and accustomed warning. Almost before the last dismal moan had ended, the anti-aircraft guns began to crash. In between their bursts I could hear the deeper, more menacing sound of bombs. It wasn't much of a raid, really, but one or two of the bombs seemed to fall too close to my room. I was reading in bed, and to drown out, or at least to take my mind off, the bombs, I reached out and turned on the radio. I was fumbling aimlessly with the dial when the room was flooded with the beauty and peace of Christmas carol music. Glorious waves of it wiped out the sound of war and conjured up visions of happier peacetime Christmases. Then the announcer spoke—in German. For it was a German station, and they were Germans who were singing those carols. Nazi bombs screaming through the air with their message of war and death; German music drifting through the air with its message of peace and salvation. When we resolve the paradox of those two sounds from a single national source, we will, at last, be in a good position to understand and solve the problem of peace and war.

SELECT BIBLIOGRAPHY

J. C. Bracq, *Evolution of French Canada* (New York, 1924).

J. B. Brebner, *North Atlantic Triangle* (Toronto, New Haven, 1945).

S. D. Clark, *The Social Development of Canada* (Toronto, 1942).

D. G. Creighton, *The Commercial Empire of the St. Lawrence* (Toronto, New Haven, 1937).

D. G. Creighton, *Dominion of the North* (Toronto, 1957).

D. G. Creighton, *John A. Macdonald: The Young Politician* (Toronto, 1952); *The Old Chieftain* (Toronto, 1955).

J. W. Dafoe, *Laurier, A Study in Canadian Politics* (Toronto, 1922).

R. M. Dawson, *Constitutional Issues in Canada, 1900-1931* (London, 1933).

R. M. Dawson, *The Government of Canada* (Toronto, 1946).

W. T. Easterbrook and H. G. J. Aitken, *Canadian Economic History* (Toronto, 1956).

R. Flenley (ed.), *Essays in Canadian History* (Toronto, 1939).

G. P. Glazebrook, *Canadian External Relations: An Historical Study to 1914* (Toronto, 1942).

G. P. Glazebrook, *A History of Transportation in Canada* (Toronto, New Haven, 1938).

M. L. Hansen and J. B. Brebner, *The Mingling of the Canadian and American Peoples* (Toronto, New Haven, 1940).

E. C. Hughes, *French Canada in Transition* (Chicago, 1943).

H. A. Innis, *The Fur Trade in Canada* (New Haven, 1930).

H. A. Innis, *Select Documents in Canadian Economic History 1497-1783* (Toronto, 1929).

H. A. Innis and A. R. M. Lower, *Select Documents in Canadian Economic History 1783-1885* (Toronto, 1933).

W. P. M. Kennedy, *The Constitution of Canada* (London, 1931).

W. P. M. Kennedy, *Statutes, Treaties and Documents of the Canadian Constitution 1713-1929* (London, 1930).

Fred Landon, *Western Ontario and The American Frontier* (Toronto, New Haven, 1941).

M. H. Long, *A History of the Canadian People,* Volume 1, New France (Toronto, 1942).

A. R. M. Lower, *Canada: Nation and Neighbour* (Toronto, 1952).

A. R. M. Lower, *Colony to Nation* (Toronto, 1946).

A. R. M. Lower, *The North American Assault on the Canadian Forest* (Toronto, New Haven, 1938).

Chester Martin, *Empire and Commonwealth* (London, 1929).

D. C. Masters, *The Rise of Toronto* (Toronto, 1947).

D. C. Masters, *The Winnipeg General Strike* (Toronto, 1950).

Edgar McInnis, *Canada: a Political and Social History* (New York, Toronto, 1947).

A. S. Morton, *History of the Canadian West to 1870-1871* (Toronto, n.d.).

W. L. Morton, *The Progressive Party in Canada* (Toronto, 1950).

Report of the Royal Commission on Dominion-Provincial Relations (the Sirois Report), volume 1 (Ottawa, 1940).

J. Holland Rose (ed.), *The Cambridge History of the British Empire,* Volume 6 (Canada) (Cambridge, England, 1930).

Adam Shortt and A. G. Doughty, *Canada and Its Provinces* (23 volumes) (Toronto, 1914).

A. Siegfried, *The Race Question in Canada* (London, 1907).

O. D. Skelton, *The Life and Letters of Sir Wilfrid Laurier* (2 volumes) (Toronto, 1921).

O. D. Skelton, *The Life and Times of Sir Alexander Tilloch Galt* (Toronto, 1920).

C. P. Stacey, *The Canadian Army 1939-1945* (Ottawa, 1948).

R. G. Trotter, *Canadian Federation* (Toronto, 1924).

Mason Wade, *The French Canadians 1760-1945* (Toronto, 1956).

W. S. Wallace, *The Dictionary of Canadian Biography* (2 volumes) (Toronto, 1945).

H. H. Walsh, *The Christian Church in Canada* (Toronto, 1956).

John S. Willison, *Sir Wilfrid Laurier and the Liberal Party, A Political History* (2 volumes) (Toronto, 1903).

INDEX